Essentials of Computer Data Files

Owen Hanson

Director of the Centre for Business Systems Analysis
The City University
London

Pitman

PITMAN PUBLISHING
128 Long Acre, London WC2E 9AN

© Owen Hanson 1985

First published in Great Britain 1985
Reprinted (with corrections) 1988

British Library Cataloguing in Publication Data
Hanson, Owen
    Essentials of computer data files.
    1. Data base management   2. System design
    3. File organization (Computer science)
    I. Title
    001.64'42   QA76.9.D3
    ISBN 0-273-02085-4

Library of Congress Cataloging in Publication Data
Hanson, Owen, 1934–
    Essentials of computer data files.
    Bibliography: p.
    Includes index.
    1. File organization (computer science). I. Title.
    QA76.9.F5H35   1985   001.64   84-25376
    ISBN 0-273-02085-4

Produced by Longman Group (FE) Limited
Printed in Hong Kong

Richard Whitwell MSc Computing Leicester Poly.
Please return here.

Contents

v

Preface

Information files lie at the core of business data processing. The replacement or enhancement of computer hardware can be carried out quite quickly. By comparison, permanent data files represent both a historical and operating record of an organization's business, and a long-term investment in data that would be difficult or impossible to recreate if it were lost. Despite this, the types of file used in business are sometimes neglected by computing course designers, and therefore there is always a demand for easily assimilated information on this subject—as the success of my first book, *Basic File Design*, showed. The present volume succeeds that book, which is now out of print, and has been written both to help students find out about real-world computing, and to provide a reference for the professional file designer.

In line with this aim, the file organization techniques discussed, and the file storage hardware described, reflect what is used in the industry. To take an example, 17 per cent of UK installations input data using punched cards[48], so they are mentioned. Sperry-Univac uses drums extensively, while many ICL and a few IBM installations still have them, so naturally drums are discussed, although most files are held on disk or tape nowadays.

Figures from surveys of file usage in the UK in 1982 and 1983 (see references 30 and 31) show the following:

71 per cent of installations use sequential files
69 per cent of installations use indexed files
33 per cent of installations use databases
32 per cent of installations use direct files
9 per cent of installations use VSAM files
2 per cent of installations use partitioned files
3 per cent of installations use all other forms of file.

The most atypical users were found to be educational establishments with only 40 per cent using sequential and 20 per cent indexed files; this is to be expected, as they tend to have large numbers of users who are learning or problem-solving. Very few production programs are run, and we teachers of computing subjects must beware of believing that our

own installations bear much resemblance to those in the business computing world. They don't, as these and similar surveys remind us.

Much of the material used here is a development of *Basic File Design*,
and some parts have appeared in articles published in *Computer Weekly*.
The author would like to thank the editorial staff of *Computer Weekly*,
ICL, NCR, CDC, STC, Honeywell, IBM (UK), IBM (Europe), Sperry-
Univac, the Datapro Research Corporation, colleagues in The City
University, IBM in the UK and Vienna, students from industry and The
City University and the many authors who have contributed to this book
with advice, comments or information. In particular, Susan K. Folkes
provided Fig. 1.1, while Norman Revell contributed the chapters on
databases and on-line systems and part of the material on security. The
book would certainly not have been written without the help of Cosette
Avakian, who found time to type it despite a very heavy day-to-day work
load; it is a great pleasure to thank her for it here.

Finally, I should like to thank my wife, daughters and friends for their
encouragement and understanding, over the period that this book has
taken to write. While to me it reflects twenty years' fascination with
information, its storage, retrieval and use, for those close to me it has
meant months of putting up with hurried and inadequate attention, due to
the demands of authorship.

Owen Hanson
The Centre for Business Systems Analysis
City University, London
August 1984

Introduction

This book is intended for readers who wish to understand the principles underlying the most commonly used file organization techniques, and the database software that has been developed using those techniques. For that reason, the hardware and software discussed reflect what is in use now in the data processing industry.

The emphasis is therefore on providing the facts needed to design efficient, cost-effective files without overloading the reader with their derivation. For those who wish to follow up a particular topic the original sources are given; anyone intending to study all of file design in depth will find *Design of Computer Data Files*[1] the most useful later reference.

Although it is hoped that the information given in the book will be of use to many types of reader, there are two categories who should find it of particular interest. These are students and file designers.

Students of systems analysis and data processing will find the book provides a brief but complete review of present data file design and practice. Designers of information files, whether writing original software or wishing to optimize manufacturers' or independently developed file handling software, will find that the essentials of the subject are presented independent of any particular manufacturer's systems.

It is assumed that the reader is already familiar with the principles and terminology of business data processing. However, the first chapter has been included for those readers who may wish quickly to refresh their knowledge of the subject before starting on the main body of the book.

The references cited in the text are listed immediately after Chapter 14, which briefly reviews them, together with other key sources, under the following headings; general, record format and handling, sequential files, direct files, indexed-sequential files, choice between file organizations, database systems, on-line systems, security, and use and performance of input-output devices. This has been done for the convenience of readers who may wish to delve further into the many specialist topics necessarily treated only briefly here.

The introduction of an important concept or term is indicated by the use of bold type. Generally, this is followed by its definition or an explanation of it. The number of the page on which it first appears, or is defined, is also shown in bold type in the index.

Questions designed to test the reader's comprehension of the subject, to provide practice in problem solving and to aid revision, are appended to each chapter (except, of course, Chapter 14).

The following abbreviations have been used throughout this book:
ms = millisecond(s);   s = second(s);   min = minute(s);   h = hour(s);
in = inch(es); kb = kilobyte(s); kc = 1000 characters; Mb = megabyte(s);
Mc = megacharacters.

1 Business applications of computers: a brief review

Introduction

In order to do any job in business or administration, you will need some data. To calculate how much somebody is paid each week or month, this data includes rate of pay, hours worked, tax rates, national insurance and pension deductions, and much else. In a manual system, this information may be taken from lists, tables, ledgers and books that are often called files. Nearly always, these files will be held in alphabetical or numerical order, so that the user can search them quickly to get the required information.

When all the business calculations in a company are carried out manually, the collection of information from files, lists, etc. will probably take less time than the actual calculation. As the number of employees in a company, the number of customers using a shop or the number of items held in stock increases, the time taken both to collect and to process (i.e. do the calculations on) this information will increase in proportion. For example, a computer can carry out calculations of the complexity involved in payroll processing at the rate of thousands of employees per second. This makes a computer a very helpful tool for a hard-worked wages clerk, whose situation is depicted in Fig 1.1.

At this stage, it is worth pointing out the essential difference between scientific and business computing. Because scientific calculations are often complicated and take a long time to complete even on a computer, the time taken to enter the data required to carry out the calculation is not very critical. That is why it is often keyed in by the user directly to the computer, and processed at once. The processing time required is long, so the program does not require new data for some time. This is different to an on-line business system, in which hundreds or even thousands of terminals may be inputting data to the computer at the same time. In general, business computing faces quite different problems. Calculations usually take a very short time, and the worst bottle-neck slowing up the preparation of payslips or invoices is entry of the data. For that reason, data is usually entered by data preparation staff, transferred into permanent data files in one process, and used to carry out some business calculation in a later process. Instead of carrying out each calculation with directly

In tray   Out tray

List of   Tax   work   Procedure
employees   tables   pad   manual

Fig. 1.1 This is a picture of the problems faced by a wages clerk who has to calculate and prepare thousands of payslips. It is used by permission of Susan K. Folkes.

entered data, all the data is prepared first, and then all the calculations are done at a later stage. A typical batch system is shown in Fig. 1.2.

Information storage

Not all the information required to carry out a business calculation is entered at the time, because that would slow up processing. In preparing invoices, for example, the name and address of a customer will hardly ever change, so it makes sense to store that information once only, and hold it permanently in the computer system, as it is then very quickly retrieved and used. The value of the goods that a customer has bought since the last invoice was sent to him will have to be entered into the system as orders are received from the customer. One way of dealing with this is to send an invoice with every order. For larger customers who would receive many invoices a day, it usually makes sense to total up all the orders for a day, a week or a month and send a single invoice for all of them. In this case, a record of all unpaid orders has to be held in the system until the next invoice is sent. This data is semipermanent, while a payment received from

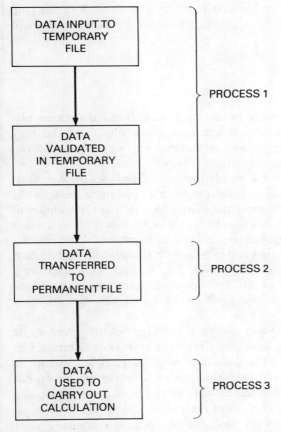

Fig. 1.2 A typical sequence in entering data into a batch processing system.

the customer will probably be processed at once to reduce their outstanding balance, and may not be held at all as a separate item.

From this, it is clear that the information required in business data processing may be 'permanent', 'semipermanent' or 'temporary'. Before it is used, this information has to be transferred into computer storage, and is usually held in a file or files. The permanent data used to run a business is of vital importance, and can be regarded as the heart of the business. Although a computer is the tool used to process business data, it is relatively easy to substitute one computer for another if it is destroyed or breaks down. By comparison, total loss of a customer file containing the names, addresses and current balance of a million customers would probably put a company out of business and certainly damage it seriously. Naturally, precautions are usually taken to prevent such loss, and we shall discuss this in Chapter 12. The speed and efficiency of a business information system can be influenced more by the optimal design and storage of information files than by the choice of computer, important though that is.

Types of data file

A file of information that is more or less permanent is called a **master file**. Examples would be personnel, customer or stock files, and the only information added would be for *new* customers, etc, while that removed would be for personnel who had left, for example.

Temporary information that is needed to record changes in payments, items in stock, price levels, etc, is usually held on an **update** or **changes file**. Changes to permanent information in a master file, such as the addition of a new employee or customer, will also be stored in an update file as the first process, and added to the master file during a later process. When such a process involves a file, it is often called a **run**—in this case an update run.

In many business applications, reference data is used. This might be a price or conversion table, or a set of descriptions. Alterations to these tend to involve changing all the data, not just some of it, and these files are often called **reference files**.

When information is no longer constantly in use, but may need to be referred to very occasionally, it is transferred to an **archive** or **historical file**. This saves embarrassment if the data is needed later, as it can still be retrieved—usually that requires a reasonable wait, however; the data is not available within the system, but has to be retrieved from a remote storage site, or at least from storage that is not on-line.

You may meet other names for files, but they usually carry out one of these functions, and these names have been used throughout the book.

The concept of data records

In a particular file, all the data that describes a given customer, stock item or employee is grouped together, and called a data **record**. Thus, in a file that contained details of 23 000 customers, there would be 23 000 records. These records may be **fixed** or **variable** in length, depending on the type of information stored. It is easy to handle fixed length records because they are all the same in size and format, but many applications require variable length information such as names, descriptions of stock items, number of shops (with addresses) owned by the customer, etc. That is because the number or size of these items is itself not fixed. For that reason, a variable length record needs to contain **pointers** to the items in it. Some computer manufacturers describe another type of record as **undefined**; this is really a variable length record, for which the user does not provide details of these pointers to the software, and so has to carry out all the recognition of items and their position in the record without help from the manufacturers' software.

Records are often **blocked**, usually to save space on a storage device or to speed up transfer of information from one device to another. We shall look at this in more detail in Chapter 4. As with individual records, blocks of records can be fixed in length—which makes it easy to tell where every record in the block starts and ends—or variable. In this case, each record usually contains a count of its own length, and the overall block contains a count of the block length, so that each record in the block can be located.

There is a limit to the number of **characters** of information that can be transferred to and from a computer system in one operation. On IBM computers this is 32 768 characters, and many systems have a more restricted size than this. If a variable length record is larger than this, it can be handled in two or more parts. Such a record is called a **spanned record**, and demands careful handling. We need not consider it further here, as the manufacturers who offer spanned records give instructions on their use. However, you need to recognize the name in case you meet it.

Data fields

Within a record, each part that holds a particular unit of information such as a customer or personnel number, a credit limit or the like, is called a **data field**. The most important of these is usually called a **key field**, or **record key**. This is the field that is used to recognize *this* record out of all the records in the file, so it has to be unique. In some cases, a record will have more than one key (*see* Chapter 8). In most cases, however, a single unique key is used to distinguish this record from all others; often it is a customer or personnel number, etc.

Each field is made up of one or more characters of data. In some circumstances, each character can hold more than one item of information—for instance, when it is a code. Usually, however, each character position holds one printable character.

A **byte** is a name used for an eight or (for Honeywell systems) nine-bit character, where each bit is a binary digit capable only of being *on* or *off*. This means that there is a maximum of $256(2^8)$ *different* bit patterns in an eight-bit byte, and 512 (2^9) in a nine-bit byte. A character can be six, eight or nine bits in size; a byte is *one form* of character, not a separate unit. You may also meet the term **word** to describe anything from 24 to 60-bit units of data that can be handled by the computer as a single entity. This is most important in scientific computing, but is also common in general-purpose computers. A word *is* a different type of unit to a character, and usually contains several characters when used to hold data to be printed, stored or moved, but only *one* item of data in a calculation.

A field or a record will be defined as taking up *n* words, bytes or characters depending on the computer being used. For most purposes, it is not necessary to analyze this in more detail.

Organization of information files

When a system is handled manually, files are almost always arranged in a meaningful sequence. For example, a telephone directory is arranged in alphabetical order. However, most of us 'guess' roughly which part of the directory to look at, and do not work through from the start of the directory page by page. In a sense, we are searching the directory *directly*.

A computer cannot 'guess' which position to jump to, so each file has to be organized in a way that suits the processing it is going to carry out. For example, if only one record in every thousand is to be processed, a sequentially organized computer file would require *every* record to be examined, even though only one per thousand is required. This has led to the development of a number of file organization techniques to optimize the use of files.

Serial files are files in no particular key order; this usually happens when records are input to the computer, to be **sorted** into a meaningful order. There are very few applications that use serial files consistently, as no one record can be located easily in the file.

Sequential files are arranged in ascending or descending key order. Any alteration to the file is identified by key, and the file is searched in sequential order until the desired record is found. In order to minimize the overall time to process *all* these alterations, they too are sorted into order before the processing run begins, so that the master file is only traversed once during the run.

When it is possible to recognize which records are required for alteration, and to avoid reading records into the computer unless they are required, the process is described as **skip-sequential processing**.

Indexed-sequential files are used when a low proportion of the records needs to be processed, either in sequence or directly. By providing an index, it is possible for the processing program to consult this index, and skip all the records that do not require processing. We shall look at the way these files can best be organized in Chapter 7.

Directly organized files are used for information that is never processed in a sequence, but always in a random fashion. This might apply for the holidays wanted by visitors to a travel agency, or the train journeys booked by passengers, for example. Here, there is little benefit in having the records stored in a given sequence. What is needed is a direct link between the **key** of the record, and its storage **address**. This can be arranged in a number of ways (*see* Chapter 6).

Inverted files are useful when no single key can be used to retrieve a record, but a combination of keys is necessary. We may wish to select a member of staff who is *both* an engineer *and* speaks German. These two attributes are used to eliminate any record that does not meet our needs, leaving us only with a choice of those that do. This is examined in Chapter 8.

Databases are growing more important as time goes on. Rather as with inverted files, they allow the user to frame an enquiry that can eliminate most or all of the unwanted data, and leave the user with a choice between a number of suitable records. Chapter 11 introduces the concepts of databases, and shows how they use the file organization techniques discussed in this book to achieve their results.

Accessing data files

However a file has been organized, it can always be accessed in three ways. These are serially, sequentially or directly.

These methods of access are more or less difficult, depending on the situation, but they are always possible. However, it should be borne in mind that any file is most efficiently referenced in the way it is organized, and sequential access to a directly organized file, or the reverse, is very inefficient.

Data file storage

An information file can be made up of many records; in some cases millions. Mainframe computers have a **main** or **immediate access storage** that can hold up to 128 million characters, although 4–16 million is more usual. For microcomputers the storage is 64 000 to 512 000 characters. Much or all of this storage is taken up by processing programs. There would perhaps be room for a small file here, but large files have to be stored on some form of additional storage, even while being processed. As data in main storage is usually lost when the computer is switched off, a permanent form of storage is required for files.

Secondary or **backing storage** is generally provided as magnetic tape, disk or (in Sperry-Univac machines) drum. The capacity of all of these is at least hundreds of millions of characters, so they are well suited to storing very large files. The characteristics of these devices very much affect file design.

File processing functions

Before a file can be processed, it has to be created. This usually involves a number of steps, which we shall review here.

In most cases, the records that make up the file will be created in electronic form by data preparation staff, reading documents that contain the required information and keying them on to magnetic tape, cassettes, floppy disks, disks or cards. A few files may be created from data that is 'captured' in some other way.

Once the information is stored in a temporary form, it is usually read onto a faster (in the sense of data transfer rate) storage device, whether magnetic disk or magnetic tape, as a serial file. One good reason for collecting the original input in this way is that it takes a long time to input all the data, and this data is probably input by a number of different people at the same time. The serial file is used to collect data from all these separate sources together. Rather than organizing sequential key input, it is more efficient to use the computer itself as a sorter.

The serial file, when it is complete, is usually sorted to create either a sequential or an indexed-sequential file. Other file types require more complicated processing.

Only after the file has been created, and the information in it checked by data control staff, is it ready for use. As the accuracy of the data making up a file is crucial—incorrect information about a customer can be worse than no information at all—the importance of the process of file creation can hardly be overemphasized. Bear in mind that this is a time when a very large volume of data has to be entered so that the opportunity for errors to occur, and the temptation not to check the data, is at its greatest.

Other terms used

Accessed   A record is *accessed* when it is examined, either to change it or to look at a given field.

Addition   A new record added to a file.

Deletion   A record that is logically removed from the file. In some systems, it is also physically removed as well. In others, it is *tagged*, meaning that a marker is set in it so it is no longer processed, and removed when the file is next *reorganized*, to clean up and optimize it.

Growth rate   A measure of the growth of the file. Note that, if additions are added but deletions are not removed, there will be an apparent growth that is greater than the real growth of the file.

Hit   When a record is accessed or processed, it is said to be hit.

Hit-rate, hit-ratio   The number of hit records as a percentage or proportion of the total records in the file.

Updated record   One that has been altered in some way.

Volatility   A measure of the change in composition of the file over a period. For any one run, it is the ratio of the sum of total additions plus total deletions to the total number of records in the file at the start of the run.

Revision questions

1   What are information files used for? Give several examples.

2   Describe in detail the information you would need to prepare an invoice for a customer. Compare the ways in which you would obtain the information to prepare it manually, and the ways in which the computer would obtain it. What files would the computer need?

3   What is the process of putting information into a permanent file?

4   Give the names of the types of data file you know of, and describe their purposes.

5   What is the difference between *accessing* and *updating* a file?

6   Describe the types of record you know of; why might they be blocked?

7   Give the names of the separate data fields you might expect to find in an employee's pay record.

8   What do you understand by the term *record key*? Give examples.

9   Distinguish between a *character*, a *byte*, and a *word*, giving the number of bits in each. What is a bit?

10   What is meant by *file organization*? How does it differ from *file access*? What file organizations do you know of? Describe their purpose.

11   Define *addition, deletion, tagging, hit, hit-rate, hit-ratio, volatility, growth rate, data file, information file*.

12   What is *immediate access storage*? How does it differ from *secondary storage*? What is the relationship of *main* and *backing storage* to these? Why have secondary storage?

13   Explain how a data file is created, in general terms, pointing out any hazards that creation presents.

14   Compare the importance of information files themselves to that of the computer used to process them.

15 What do information files represent to a business? Justify any statements or comments that you make.

16 Define the term *run*. How many runs would you expect to be needed in the creation of a sequential file? Justify your answer.

17 Why would you expect a record key to be unique? How is this affected when you are dealing with information retrieval in a library?

2 Storage devices

The capacity of main storage is limited, and a significant number of programs will be active at any time and so need storage space. For this reason, computer systems have always relied on the availability of secondary storage in order to hold large data files.

Magnetic tape

In the mid-1950s, two methods of secondary storage were in use. The main one was magnetic tape, handled rather as in a tape recorder. Tapes are typically 2400 ft long, about half an inch wide and $1\frac{1}{2}$ thousandths of an inch thick. The **base** of the tape is made of Mylar plastic, and on this is laid an overlay of ferric, chromic or mixed oxides, held together by a binder, to record data.

The base, or substrate, determines the amount of stretch in the tape. The quality of the coating decides the 'signal-to-noise' ratio, and so the sensitivity of the tape to data recording. The binder affects generation of magnetic dust, which is created in the unit itself due to contact between the tape and the read/write heads and leads to misread errors, etc. Slitting of the tape can affect feeding and winding of the tape in subsequent operations.

From all this, you can see that tape will need careful treatment if it is to give good results. A section through a tape is shown in Fig. 2.1, and details of recording and operation are given in Figs 2.2 and 2.3.

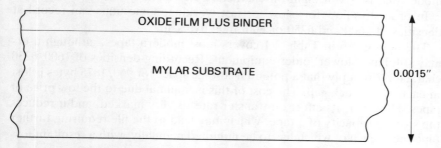

Fig. 2.1 Section through a magnetic tape.

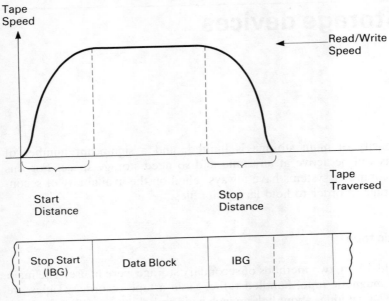

Fig. 2.2 The relationship between read–write operations and the size of inter-block gaps on magnetic tapes.

In analyzing a tape for storage purposes, we shall be looking at its transfer rate in characters (or bytes) per second, the time taken to traverse the inter-block gap (IBG), the density with which data is recorded and (less important) the rewind time. The figures for a number of IBM tapes are given in Table 2.1.

Because there are still many organizations using seven-track archive tapes, a number of these units can be run in either seven or nine-track mode (that is, six or eight-bit characters plus a parity bit).

In order to allow for 'slow' or fast working, some units can record at densities of 1600 and 6250 or 800/1600 bytes/in.

The data given in Table 2.1 covers most modern tapes, although users may still have slower, older equipment. Recording densities of 1600/6250 characters/in imply that a potential storage space for 960/1875 bytes is lost in each inter-block gap. The cost of this is minimal due to the low price of tapes. However, its effect on transfer rates is very marked, and it reduces the storage capacity of a tape, which may lead to the file requiring further tape reels, each of which has to be mounted manually, with a resultant loss of time.

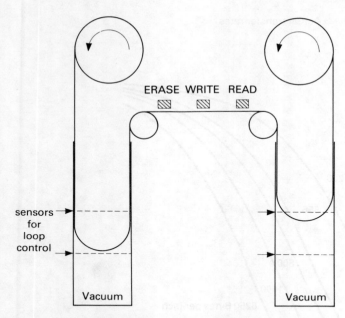

Fig. 2.3 A simplified diagram of a conventional tape drive, showing vacuum loops, loop control and read, write and erase heads.

Table 2.1 IBM tape performance data.

IBM number	Transfer rate (kb)	IBG time (ms)		Rewind time (s)	Recording density (bytes/in)
3420–3	60/120	(10.0†)	8.0	60	800/1600
3420–4	120/470	8.0	(4.0*)	60	1600/6250
3420–5	100/200	(6.0†)	4.0	60	800/1600
3420–6	200/780	4.0	(2.4*)	60	1600/6250
3420–7	160/320	(3.75†)	3.0	45	800/1600
3420–8	320/1250	3.0	(1.5*)	45	1600/6250
8809 Start–stop	20 kb	6.0		160	1600
Streaming mode	160 kb	48.0		160	1600

* = 6250 bytes/in operation
† = Seven-track operation (non return to zero IBM recording mode)
Nine-track operation uses phase-encoded or group-coded recording for improved reliability

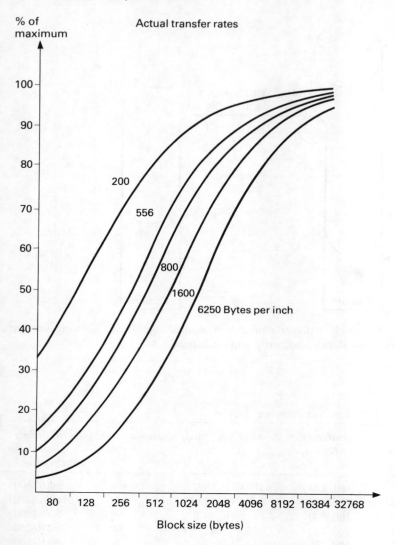

Fig. 2.4 Tape drive performance showing the improvement in actual transfer rates that is obtained by using large data blocks.

Transfer rates specified are always maxima. They are reduced by the time taken to traverse inter-block gaps, as shown in Fig. 2.4. The curves given are based on an inter-block gap of 0.6 in for 1600 bytes/in tapes and 0.3 in for 6250 bytes/in tapes; these are typical. They also assume that the inter-block gap is traversed at an average speed that is the same as that required for reading, which again is often the case.

No transfer speed is given as, if the assumptions made above are valid, these curves hold for all transfer speeds. They give an indication of the effect of block size on transfer speed and it is clear that, unless record sizes are large, the actual transfer rates will be much lower than the figures quoted by manufacturers.

The curves given assume that a further tape read instruction is issued in time to avoid the tape drive mechanism stopping. If it does stop, the waste of time is greater. For example, a Univac Uniservo 16 will traverse a gap in 5.0 ms, so long as the next read instruction is given in time, but a physical start–stop will take 8.0 ms. Corresponding figures for the Uniservo 20 are 3.0 and 5.0 ms respectively.

The effect of record size on the length of tape required is the inverse of its effect on actual transfer rates. For example, if the actual transfer rate is 25 per cent of the figure given by the manufacturer, the file will take up four times as much space on tape as it would do if there were no gaps at all. (This only applies precisely if the inter-block gap is traversed at the reading speed. However, it gives a good estimate even when that does not apply). The effect of IBGs on tape capacity is shown in Fig. 2.5.

Magnetic tape is a serial medium, in that a desired record can only be reached by first traversing all other records between it and the read heads. This affected the design of all computer systems in the 1950s; however, tape still provides efficient and useful storage today, so long as it is carefully used and maintained, for applications that suit its mode of operation. See references 46, 47 for further details.

The average response time of a tape system to an enquiry will be about 1 min. This may be satisfactory for a single enquiry, but not for a large number, and it means the normal sequential processing run must be interrupted to service the enquiry.

Many data processing jobs require a much faster response than one enquiry a minute; some of these are enquiry-only systems (often seat booking of some sort), while others need a mixture of sequential processing and enquiries. This last might be based on regular updates of, say, car insurance records when premiums are due, and reference to a particular record after an accident. To meet this type of need, a number of direct-access devices have been developed.

Direct-access devices

Physically, there are three types of device: drum, mass storage device and disk.

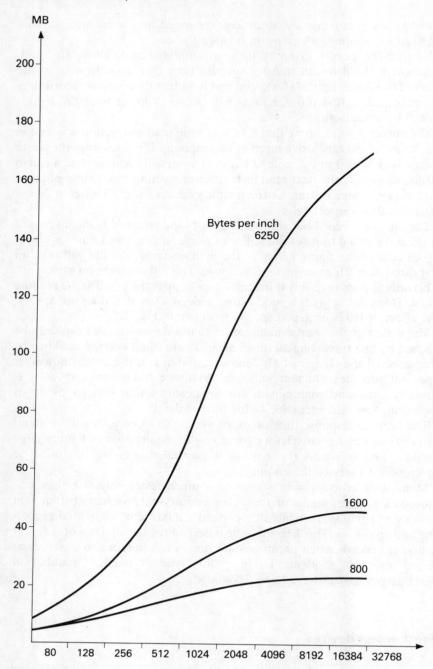

Fig. 2.5 Storage capacity of 2400 ft tapes for various block sizes.

Drums

Sperry-Univac was the last company to offer these on their computers, but you may meet them in older installations. Information is stored on the surface of a metal drum coated with an iron oxide film which can be magnetized. The drum rotates and the data is written on to, or read off from, circular 'tracks' round the circumference of the cylinder by read–write heads. There is one head per track and the heads are usually arranged in groups around the drum, e.g. the first group of heads read tracks 1, 9, 17, etc . . ., the second group read tracks 2, 10, 18 . . ., and the eighth group read tracks 8, 16, 24 . . .. All the information on the drum is available in a single rotation of the drum. Drums are usually fixed, that is, only one storage surface is available. They often need a long running time (about 2 h) to clear all magnetic dust from the surface after they have been switched on, and a lot of power to run. They were a limited alternative to tape in the 1950s, and were used until recently because of their rapid access times, but few are in use now that disks have overtaken their transfer rate, while providing greater capacity.

Mass-storage devices

In most of these devices, data is held on cartridge tapes that can be stored in a 'honeycomb' structure for later retrieval. A cartridge can be selected by a data access mechanism that reads it onto a magnetic disk—this process is usually known as **staging**. This provides the ability to retrieve any item of data from a total volume of up to 472 000 000 000 bytes in an average time of 8–13 s (these figures apply to the IBM 3850 mass-storage facility). These devices provide relatively slow direct access, but they offer massive data storage capacity at low cost, with some enquiry facilities.

The Braegen Automated Tape Library is what it says—an automatic mounting and storage system for conventional magnetic tapes. Table 2.2 gives values of capacity and data access times for three of these devices.

Table 2.2   Mass-storage devices.

	Braegen 7110 ATL	*IBM 3850*	*CDC 38500*
Capacity range (bytes)	802 to 7808 (thin reels) 144 360 000 000 to 1 405 440 000 000	35 000 000 000 to 472 000 000 000	16 000 000 000 to 1 000 000 000 000
Data access (s)	15 to 20 to mount	8 to 13 to access	7.5 average to access

The mass-storage device figures in Table 2.2 show that these have enormous capacity, but provide relatively slow access. As they are not suitable for rapid access, they are extensively used for applications such as insurance files, where enquiries are few and far between and sequential updates are also required.

Disks

Information is stored on concentric 'tracks' on the surface of magnetic disks. **Removable disks** are usually arranged in groups of six or 11, each vertically above the other. The group spins on its axis as a single pack. The top surface of the top disk and the bottom surface of the bottom disk are not used for recording, so there are ten or 20 usable surfaces per track. Non-removable disks—with up to 100 surfaces—are also used. They are called **fixed disks**, and now represent the major part of disk production.

Data is retrieved or written by read–write heads, one per surface, which are connected together to form an access 'comb'. Information on any surface can be retrieved by head movement to the required track, followed by rotation of the pack until the record required is under the head. The arrangement is shown in Fig. 2.6.

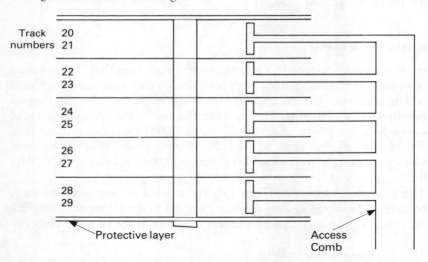

Fig. 2.6 Storage of sequential files on consecutive tracks of a cylinder.

One might expect that it would be sensible to fill a disk with data, starting with the first track on the top surface and using all the tracks on that surface in order, before going on to the second surface. This is not done, because it would mean that in sequential processing the access comb would have to move at the end of reading each single track. Instead, the first track on a disk is the outer track on the top surface, the second is the outer track on the second surface, and so on. All the outer tracks make up one **cylinder**, and as these tracks can be read or written without head movement, it is better to think of a pack being made up of cylinders rather than tracks and surfaces.

Device performance and uses

When discussing the performance of these devices, we have to know three figures. These are the **access time**, or time to get to any desired record; the **maximum capacity** of the device in bytes (eight-bit characters) or characters; and the **rate** at which information is transferred from the device to the CPU or vice versa. These figures are given for some typical devices in Tables 2.3 and 2.4. (Note that modern disks are all fixed.)

Table 2.3 Removable disks.

IBM number	Transfer rate/s	Capacity	Access times (ms)		
			min	avg	max
1311	50 kc†	2 Mc		160	
2311	156 kb**	7 Mb*	25	75	135
2314	312 kb	28 Mb	25	75	135
3330–1	806 kb	100 Mb	10	30	55
3330–11	806 kb	200 Mb	10	30	55
3340*	885 kb	70 Mb	10	25	50

*See note below Table 2.4;
†kc = 10^3 characters;
**kb = 10^3 bytes;
Mc = 10^6 characters;
Mb = 10^6 bytes

Table 2.4 Fixed disks.

IBM number	Transfer rate/s	Capacity		Access times (ms)		
				min	avg	max
3344*	0.885 Mb	280	Mb	10	25	50
3350*	1.198 Mb	317.5	Mb	10	25	50
3310*	1.031 Mb	64.5	Mb		27	
3370*	1.859 Mb	285	Mb	5	20	40
3375*	1.859 Mb	409.85	Mb		19	
3380*	3.0 Mb	630	Mb	3	16	

* Winchester Technology disks. The heads and disks of these devices are permanently sealed, to prevent dirt or contamination affecting them. The technique was developed at Hursley Manor, near Winchester, England. Hence the name.

Magnetic disks are often removable, meaning that the total storage on-line at one time is as shown here, but that for sequential processing the storage capacity is not limited. Disks are available with a very wide range of access time, capacity and transfer rate, and as they are operationally more satisfactory than the other devices they are tending to supersede them.

Data recording

On disk, drum or mass storage device (except the Braegen), a character is recorded as a serial string of bits around a track, each bit on or off as in the character held in main storage. The parity bit, which is an additional bit attached to each byte of data in the computer, and is recorded as a ninth bit of each byte on magnetic tape, is not stored on disk. Instead, check bytes are added at the end of each complete field of data. The control unit of the device thus accepts a complete character of information in parallel, takes off the parity bit, passes it on to the device as a string of bits and, when the last data character has passed, adds the check field to it.

Two methods of record storage are in common use. The first is **sector mode**. Some ICL systems provide the user with a track that is permanently divided into a number of record-containing fields, each able to hold 512 characters of six bits. The user can choose, logically, to handle these records in ones, twos, fours or eights, i.e. to store records in 'buckets' of 512, 1024, 2048 or 4096 characters capacity. However small the records, the minimum size of storage bucket is 512 characters, and records must be blocked together to use the available space sensibly. Most floppy disks, microcomputer 'hard' disks and IBM's 3310 and 3370 devices use a fairly similar sector system.

Most IBM devices leave the choice of record (or block) size to the user. Table 2.5 shows the effect of record size on the number of records stored per track for a number of IBM devices. The total amount of data stored on a track is at its greatest if the whole track is used as a single large record or block, while the use of, say, five-byte records cuts the data stored on a track to a small fraction of its potential capacity.

This loss of useful data storage is due to the extra control fields required for each record, and the extra inter-record and inter-control field gaps that are required.

Records may be stored either 'with' keys (e.g. account numbers, personnel numbers etc.) or 'without'. These two formats are shown in Fig. 2.7. Of course, in a record 'without' its key, the key has to be included in the data part of the record, to identify this record within the file.

Although a number of other control fields are used in most manufacturers' disk formats, Fig. 2.7 shows the essential difference between the two types of record.

The gap between the key field and the data field gives sufficient time for a comparison to be made between the record key and a desired key, held in

Table 2.5   The relationship between number of blocks per track and the total data stored on a track for a number of disk devices.

Maximum bytes per physical record formatted without keys				Physical records per track	Maximum bytes per physical record formatted with keys			
2314	3330	3380*	2305 Mod.2		2314	3330	3380*	2305 Mod.2
7294	13030	47 476	14 660	1	7249	12974	47 220	14 569
3521	6447	23 476	7 231	2	3476	6391	23 220	7 140
2298	4253	15 476	4 754	3	2254	4197	15 220	4 663
1693	3156	11 476	3 516	4	1649	3100	11 220	3 425
1332	2498	9 076	2 773	5	1288	2442	8 820	2 682
1092	2059	7 476	2 278	6	1049	2003	7 220	2 187
921	1745	6 356	1 924	7	878	1689	6 100	1 833
793	1510	5 492	1 659	8	750	1454	5 236	1 568
694	1327	4 820	1 452	9	650	1271	4 564	1 361
615	1181	4 276	1 287	10	571	1125	4 020	1 196
550	1061	3 860	1 152	11	506	1005	3 604	1 061
496	962	3 476	1 040	12	452	906	3 220	949
450	877	3 188	944	13	407	821	2 932	853
411	805	2 932	863	14	368	749	2 676	772
377	742	2 676	792	15	333	686	2 420	701
347	687	2 484	730	16	304	631	2 228	639
321	639	2 234	676	17	277	583	2 068	585
298	596	2 164	627	18	254	540	1 908	536
276	557	2 004	584	19	233	501	1 748	493
258	523	1 876	544	20	215	467	1 620	453
241	491	1 780	509	21	198	435	1 524	418
226	463	1 684	477	22	183	407	1 428	386
211	437	1 588	448	23	168	381	1 332	357
199	413	1 492	421	24	156	357	1 236	330
187	391	1 396	396	25	144	335	1 140	305
176	371	1 332	373	26	133	315	1 076	282
166	352	1 268	352	27	123	296	1 012	261
157	336	1 204	332	28	114	279	948	241
148	318	1 140	314	29	105	262	884	223
139	303	1 076	297	30	96	247	820	206

* The 3380 shows data record length only, for keys of 1–20 bytes. For 21–52 byte keys, each data record is 32 bytes shorter, and so on in 32 byte increments of the key length

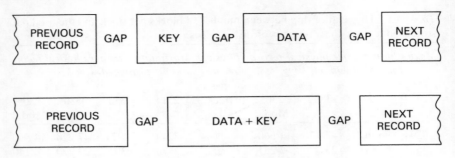

Fig. 2.7 The two possible record formats on disk: 'with' and 'without' keys.

the control unit, and allows the record to be read into main storage if it is the desired record. If it is not, the search continues until the required record key is found. Time is not lost reading unwanted records into main storage before checking them, as would have happened if the second ('without key') format had been used. For sequential file processing, this means that unwanted records can be 'skipped'; the process is called **skip-sequential processing**. For indexed-sequential and direct processing, it again allows only wanted records to be read into main storage, without the need for an index to identify these records. This compares with the sector mode of addressing, for which an index will usually be required.

The total amount of useful data that can be stored on a track for each of these formats, and various numbers of records per track, is shown in Table 2.5. The effect of number and size of records on storage capacity of disk is given in Fig. 2.8. This shows that for a disk, as distinct from a tape, bigger record size is not always better.

This emphasizes that it is vital to choose appropriate blocking factors, particularly for large blocks.

The manufacturers usually provide tables and formulae that the user can employ to estimate the effect of any given blocking factor chosen. Figure 2.8 underlines the meaning of these tables, and the user may find it helpful to construct one for his own devices.

Disks do not have a direct equivalent of the tape start–stop time, in that the gap between two records will be traversed in about 0.025–0.1 ms, and the disk spins constantly, so avoiding start–stops. However, this very rapid transition from one record to the next makes it likely that the next record will be available before it is required; much of this book concentrates on ways of avoiding or reducing the loss of time that results if this happens.

Methods of exploiting the many possibilities for disk system design, using multiple channels, channel switches, control units and multiple data paths are described in detail in reference 46.

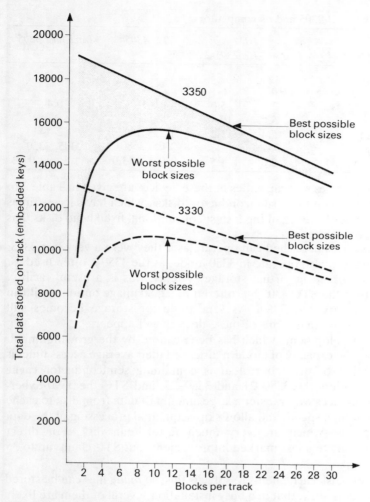

Fig. 2.8   The effect of block sizes on the amount of data that can be stored on a disk track.

Alternatives to disk

For many years, fixed head disks, in which there is one or more heads per track, have been in use. The fact that there is at least one head for every track has reduced **average access time** from around 24.33 ms for the 3380 (including rotational delay) to 2.5 and 5.0 ms for the 2305 models 1 and 2.

This is ideal for the storage of tables, operating system transient routines, virtual storage pages and the like. However, recently a competitor to these devices has appeared, in semiconductor 'disks'. The access

Table 2.6 The IBM 2305 and its competitors.

	IBM 2305-1	IBM 2305-2	STC 4305	Intel Fast 3805
Access time (ms)				
Minimum	0	0	—	—
Average	2.5	5.0	0.3	0.4
Maximum	5.0	10.0	—	—
Capacity (Mb)	5.4	11.2	11.25–192	11.2–144
Compatibility	—	—	2305, 3380	2305, 3350
Transfer rate (Mb/s)	3.0	1.5	1.0, 1.5 or 3.0	1.5 to 4.0

speeds, transfer rates and capacities of these devices are given in Table 2.6. User experience with these semiconductor 'disks', which have access times about seven times lower than the fastest conventional fixed head disks, has been very favourable.

Both the devices described can operate as if they were a very fast 2305. The Intel 3805 can also operate in 3350 mode; as the 3350 is often used for page dataset storage in virtual storage systems, this is a useful facility. From May 1984 the STC 4305 has offered the 3380 image option, so it can be used as a very fast 3380. As semiconductor storage becomes still cheaper, it is likely that more of these devices will appear.

A further development, which has been caused by the growing imbalance between the capacity of modern disks and their average access time, is the introduction of disk control units containing semiconductor **cache storage**. IBM offers the 3880–21 and 3880–23, and STC the 3390 Sybercache. These devices will transfer a large amount of data from disk to cache sequentially at high speed, and allow skip-sequential processing of the data at cache speeds—which are very much faster than disk. For direct reference they make a less marked improvement, but STC claim 'up to 35 per cent'.

The problem disk cache helps to solve is this: so *many* files can be stored on a large modern disk, that in a busy installation several of them are likely to be in use at any one time. This leads to **head contention**. The read–write heads can only be in one place at a time, and other files have to wait. In serious cases, the performance of the whole system can be very gravely reduced by this weakness of having disks with a volume storage capacity that their access times are not fast enough to support. The result is almost certain to be the introduction of more disk cache to help ease this balance.

Amdahl Corporation has significantly decided *not* to follow the greater volume path taken by IBM with its 635 Mb volumes of data on the 3380. Amdahl's 6280 disks each offer the same volume as a 3350 disk—317.5 Mb. However, by providing faster access than the 3350, and more paths to the data than the 3380, these disks are claimed to give a better performance than either for on-line processing.

A new type of device is just appearing on the market for archiving purposes. Evaluation versions of Shugart's Optimem 1000 **optical disks**, and the Philips and CDC equivalents, are now entering service. These devices record data permanently by forming pits in a suitable disk surface using a laser beam. The data is read by a low-energy laser beam; this has the advantage that dirt, scratches etc.—within reason—do not affect reading. However, the data is permanent, which limits the application of these devices.

Capacity of the optical disks available at present ranges from 1 gigabyte (1000 Mb) to 4 gigabytes. Transfer rates are from 250 kb/s to 3 Mb/s, while head movements and delays due to disk rotation average 3 to 6 times the equivalent for magnetic disks. We can expect to see considerable improvement in optical disk performance in the near future, with a resulting increase in their use.

Conclusion

In designing information files, the devices on which the information will be stored have to be considered. Fast though these devices seem, they are orders of magnitude slower than main storage, and unless the file designer takes their properties and mode of operation into account, they can hold up processing very severely. We shall look at the ways their weaknesses can be avoided, and their strengths used, in the following chapters.

Revision questions

1   Why are data files usually held on secondary storage?

2   Describe the make-up of magnetic tape. How do you think the reeling of tape tightly into a spool affects the life of recorded data? What are the likely sources of magnetic dust in a tape unit? What other factors do you think might affect tape performance?

3   What figures would we need to be given in order to decide if a given tape unit was suitable for a particular job?

4   Why do many tape units offer both seven and nine-track operation? What does this tell us about how quickly users transfer data to new media?

5   Explain why tapes are not used for enquiry systems.

6   How many types of direct-access device do you know of? Describe them.

7   What do you think now limits the use of magnetic drum storage?

8   When would you wish to use a mass storage device? Give a typical application of these devices.

9   What is the 'cylinder' concept on disk? Why and how is it applied?

10   Which figures do we need to know, in assessing the use of a direct-access device?

11   What do you think to be the pros and cons of having removable disk storage? Why have the manufacturers moved away from this type of storage?

12   How is data recorded on disk? What formats are you aware of? What are the advantages of each format, and hence when would you use them?

13   Do you know of any new alternatives to disk? If so, why do you think they were developed?

14   For what particular jobs are semiconductor 'disks' very suitable?

15   Why have disk cache devices appeared recently? What alternative might have reduced the need for them?

16   What is 'head contention'? Suggest a number of ways of reducing or eliminating it.

17   Why do we need to consider the performance of secondary storage devices when we design information files?

18   What effect does increasing the size of data blocks on tape have on: storage capacity; transfer rate; number of tapes required for a large file? Would you say a bigger block size is better?

19   Compare the effect of increasing the size of block on any *one* disk device for which figures are given in Table 2.2, with the effect on tape. What conclusion do you draw with regard to block size? With disk, what other considerations do you have to take into account?

3 Choice of file organization

In deciding on the way a file should be organized, the designer will aim to provide the user with the facilities required while taking up the minimum computer time and storage.

A number of factors have to be taken into account. They include reference facility, activity, volatility, size, growth and security/back up.

Reference facility

The user may require a direct service, for example for airline bookings, or bank account queries. However, input is often batched naturally; an example of this is payments, which will arrive with the morning and afternoon mail. In such cases, the user may wish for 'immediate' service, but it usually pays to batch and sort rather than to process updates directly. The file designer must clearly agree with the user what reference facility is to be provided before starting to design the file.

Activity

Broadly this means the percentage of records updated on each run. It is affected by the hit ratio—defined as the number of records accessed divided by the total records in the file—and also by the fan in/out ratio, which measures the number of times any record is accessed in a given run. In the file design stage, activity is usually not yet known for a master file. An exception to this is a payroll file, where the activity is usually known precisely, and is often 100 per cent. For transaction, print and similar files, it is normally 100 per cent. As activity affects file organization more than most other factors, statistics should be accumulated to review the file design adopted at a specified time after the file goes into service, with a view to changing the method of setting up and processing the file if this proves necessary.

Volatility

This is the percentage of records added to or deleted from a file during a run. It only degrades files that are updated in place; as most magnetic tape files are copied during processing, volatile files are well suited to storage on tape. Files stored on direct access devices, on the other hand, will require a lot of spare space to accommodate additions if these are numerous, and will continue to carry an overhead of deleted records until the next reorganization, unless these records are removed on each run.

Although some software does remove deleted records, this adds to run times and housekeeping overheads, so the user pays a price for storing a volatile file on a direct access device, however the situation is handled.

Size

A very large file may exceed the available direct access storage in an installation; insurance or banking files are often stored on mass storage devices of very high capacity, because they require a direct access capability and also have to be processed sequentially. Although modern, large capacity disk storage devices can hold this volume of data, they are relatively expensive and often provide much more rapid data handling capacity than is necessary for the insurance application concerned. If such a device is available, it should be used for more suitable tasks.

A small sequential file may be stored on a direct-access device to avoid frequent mounting and dismounting of tapes. If such files are stored on tape, they present a problem because of the little space they require. Storing a number of small files on the same tape leads to extra tape processing time, as the operating system will have to space through all the files on the tape until it finds the required data file. In addition, control of file availability becomes more difficult, as authorization of the issue of one file to the operations staff means that all the files on the tape can be processed. This may present a security hazard.

When files are neither very large nor very small, size is likely mainly to affect the blocking factor chosen.

Growth

This may be linked to volatility; however, if steady growth is expected, e.g. in a library, then file design must take account of future size rather than just accommodate the present data. Growth is particularly important in the design of direct files, and is discussed in more detail on p. 70.

Security/backup

Magnetic tape is more prone to errors than direct access devices. However, the copying of tape during processing provides backup during every run.

Disks need to be copied, usually to tape, as an extra operation. Depending on the level of security required,[42] costs may become very high. This will be reflected in file design and may influence the choice of device or file organization. This is taken further in Chapter 12.

Table 3.1   The relationship between the most important factors affecting a file and the type of organization that may be chosen.

Required reference	Activity	Volatility	Size	File organization indicated
Sequential only	Low Medium High	Low is suitable for direct access files, high for magnetic tape	Large favours magnetic tape. small, direct access	Sequential disk file Either Magnetic tape file
Sequential only—very high speed transfer	Any	Only suitable if low	Any	Specialist sequential disk file
Sequential with a little direct access	Low is suitable for direct access devices, high for magnetic tape		Not relevant	Usually sequential disk using a binary chop search. If very little direct access, could be on magnetic tape
Sequential with significant direct access	An indexed sequential file will be more likely to be batch processed the higher the activity (less delay and more arm movement saved)	Low reduces overflow area provision (but watch the evenness of the update pattern). High implies a loosely packed high overflow file	If small, reduces importance of design decisions. If large, makes them more vital	An indexed file on direct access. If file is large, e.g. insurance and infrequently accessed, use mass storage devices, with indexes on faster smaller direct access devices. If small, store indexes in main storage if possible.
Direct with a little sequential access	Not relevant, as each record is handled as a separate item.	If low, use a packing density of 80%–90% depending on the statistics available. If high, provide more space for additional records	Not relevant	Direct file. For sequential usage an 'index' file in sequential order, with key + the disk address as data provides maximum efficiency
Direct only	Not relevant	Not relevant	Not relevant	A direct file
Library	Not relevant	Not relevant	Not relevant	Specialist files
Production management etc.	Not relevant	Not relevant	Not relevant	Specialist files

When these factors have been determined, the designer will decide what type of file is required. Table 3.1 sets out the relationship between the most important factors given above and the file organization that is indicated by their combination in any given case. This does not cover the field exhaustively, nor is the 'indicated' file always the best. Table 3.1 provides a starting point, and also a method of checking the organization of a long-established file.

Design review

Reviewing the design and performance of files already in operation should be standard procedure. Statistics on actual file usage will often show that the design assumptions were incorrect, and a review of design may allow direct-access space to be saved, response time to be improved, etc. Simple measures such as reducing or increasing the frequency of runs can lead to a marked saving in tape passing time; a different type of update—perhaps skip sequential on disk rather than a low activity tape file—may also pay dividends. These points are expanded in the chapters dealing with particular file types.

Revision questions

1 What does the file designer intend to achieve in choosing a particular file organization for a given file?

2 Explain the factors that will influence the designer in deciding on the most suitable organization for a particular file.

3 Discuss the effect of file size on choice of file organization.

4 What file organization would you choose for a volatile file, and why?

5 Name three types of file that you would expect to show 100 per cent activity, and explain why.

6 Specify types of file that would naturally require direct access facilities. Contrast these with any that seem naturally suited to batching and sorting.

7 Explain why the design of a file should be reviewed at intervals, and what might be gained by doing this.

8 Draw up a table tracing the types of file organization most suitable for: sequential reference only; sequential with some direct access; direct access with some sequential; direct only.

9   In what respect are sequential, indexed-sequential and direct files a sequence? How would you decide between them? When is none of them suitable?

10 Why bother with choice of file organization, when indexed-sequential files can meet almost all needs?

11 Explain when sequential file organization is clearly indicated. Compare it with the situation when indexed sequential organization is the obvious choice. What would be the deciding factors at the transition between the two?

12 In what circumstances would you recommend a directly organized file? Explain why, and when, you would decide on an indexed sequentially organized file instead.

4 The influence of record format on design

Introduction

Record format has an effect both on the processing time and input–output (I/O) handling time required for a record. These times should be minimized wherever possible, and in cases where reducing one increases the other, a balance has to be struck between them; altering the record format can assist in this.

Input–output time is made up of

1. locating the required record;
2. transferring the record into main storage (or out of it).

The first of these can often be overlapped with processing, but the second will occupy a device, control unit and channel for some time, and will also require main storage cycles to read the record into storage.

Processing time consists of

1. record processing;
2. housekeeping (blocking/deblocking, locating fields, moving updated fields into the record etc).

Neither I/O nor processing time can be avoided entirely, but each can be reduced by correct design. The factors that can be altered include record length, the fixed or variable form of records, the layout of the data and any blocking factors used.

If a job is to be run on its own—not usual in modern systems—record format can be adjusted to achieve a **balanced run**, in which I/O and central processor times are equal. Record length, layout, etc, can be manipulated to improve the slower processing constituent, I/O or processor, at the expense of the other and so achieve this balance.

In a multiprogramming situation a mix of jobs will include some that are central-processor bound, some I/O bound and others that are balanced. It is no longer important to balance each program; the emphasis changes to minimizing and balancing the total I/O and processor times of all the programs being run at a given time.

In contrast with single programs, where balancing can mean that it pays to allow a marked loss in efficiency of, say, I/O timing to achieve a small saving in central processor time, multiprogramming systems should concentrate only on changes that give rise to overall improvement.

The factors that can be adjusted are examined in more detail below.

Record length

Many of the fields in a record are of known size. Others, such as name and address or outstanding transaction fields, vary from record to record. If space is not a problem, these can each be of the maximum size required for the data; this will mean some wasted space in most records, but will retain a fixed format. Ideally, there should also be some spare space left in each record to allow for future changes.

The price of opting for fixed length records, with or without room for expansion, is that the total file will be larger than is absolutely necessary. Usually this implies an increased record transfer time in proportion to increased record size.

If this extra length also causes the file to spill on to a second or further reel of tape, or increases card records to more than 80 characters, then there might be good reason to cut record size to a minimum. For example, a new reel of tape will involve a rewind and remount operation, or the use of an extra tape drive. In the same way, an extra card per record could double file size and so greatly increase record read time.

Occasionally, however, increased length can *reduce* processing time. In Fig. 4.1, records are shown on a disk track. If the processing time for a

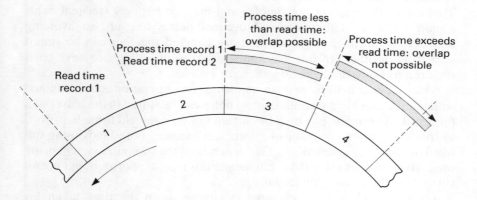

Fig. 4.1 If processing time exceeds read time, only one record can be read per I/O buffer on each revolution. Reduction of processing time or increase of read time (by lengthening the record) can avoid lost revolutions.

block is longer than its read time, several revolutions of the disk will be needed to process the whole track. Lengthening the block, so that one block can be processed while another is read in, will balance the position and avoid wasted time due to extra disk revolutions.

Fixed or variable format

Whenever space in main or backing storage is limited, variable-length records may be a solution. However, this will automatically increase housekeeping time, as fields will have to be located from data held at the front of the record (which will be fixed in format), checked for length, etc. For this reason, a variable format should only be used if marked savings in I/O time justify it. If many fields can be dropped from a large number of records in a large file, then variable format should pay.

It is best to restrict the number of variable record types to two or three—a header with one or two additional areas. This will limit the housekeeping time needed to separate and identify the various data fields. When relatively few blocks of a large file are being processed and the file is obviously I/O bound, variable-length records should be considered, but this format should always be used with care.

Record layout

If space is available, name and address fields can be held edited in the record, and so require only a move before printing. Codes, which were probably input originally in alphanumeric format, should be held in binary. This makes boolean testing simpler and may save space. Decimal fields should be held so that assumed decimal points line up, so avoiding unnecessary shifting; and fields that are handled together can be stored next to each other. In this way, moves that would otherwise have been required to bring the fields together are avoided.

When a given field is used on its own in one operation, but combined with another field in a second, the two fields can be stored in the halves of a full word. Arithmetic can then be carried out on one field using half-word instructions, and comparisons or sorts can examine both fields using full word or character instructions. This depends on the computer system being used. IBM systems using BAL can handle this type of approach, but not all current machines have this facility.

Record layout is most effective in cutting down the time taken for central-processor bound jobs, and runs that are long or frequently used. Some of these ideas are useful even if the job is I/O bound, but in this case they should not involve lengthening the record.

Optimum blocking factor

Records are blocked to save time in accessing and reading data, or to save space on backing storage. When a record is requested by a program, the delay before it is available is the sum of the time required to locate the record and the time to read it in. The transfer rates quoted for secondary storage only allow for the second of these. Actual transfer rates are always slower; the larger the data block, the smaller this reduction.

A tape start–stop time is usually 2 to 10 ms. (The figures are given in Table 2.1.) As 2000–12 500 characters could be read in this time, it is obviously important to reduce the number of blocks, and so the start–stop times, to a minimum. Disk head movement and track search times are even greater, so the reduction in actual transfer rate is higher, and blocking can yield marked improvements for disk processing too.

Magnetic tape is very cheap, so the cost of the tape saved by blocking is not significant. However, if the need for an extra reel can be avoided, this will save a tape change that can take 5 min including rewind time, or the use of a second tape unit.

Blocking records correctly on a direct access device will allow more records to be on-line at the same time. Whether the user has bucket formatted disks, or is able to use any record size on a track, poorly chosen blocking factors are wasteful. On an IBM 3330 disk subsystem for example, eight 1400 byte blocks can be stored with embedded keys per track. Only two 4200 bytes can be held per track, however, as this block size is just too large for efficient use of the track (three × 4197 blocks can be stored, but three × 4200 overlap). In such a case, the use of a larger blocking factor wastes space. Figure 4.2 emphasizes this point. (*See also* Fig. 2.8.)

The costs of blocking are main-storage space and transfer time.

Main-storage space. Larger blocks use more space; if it is available, this is not a drawback. Usually, there is competition for space in the central processor, and the designer has to decide whether blocking makes the best use of it. For a master file used by several programs, each will have a certain amount of space for data blocks. The final block size chosen will be that imposed by the smallest space available in any of these programs, even if it reduces efficiency in other programs.

Transfer time As block size increases, so does the time to read a block. For magnetic tape this is not important, because the whole file will be read in any case. For direct access devices, it can be wasteful. A sequential file in which only one record in every hundred is processed gives the figures shown in Table 4.1. Figure 4.3 presents this relationship in a form that can

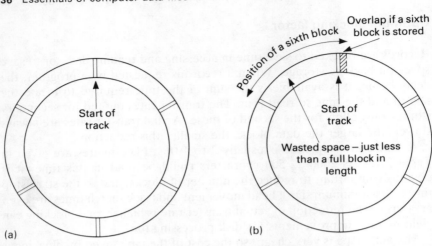

Fig. 4.2 The choice of suitable block sizes on disk is affected by the track storage capacity. (a) In this case, six blocks fit exactly on a track and no data storage space is wasted. (b) In this case, the six blocks just overlap, so only five can be stored on the track. Almost a sixth of the track is wasted.

be used to calculate the effects of blocking on the activity of files in general. More comprehensive data is given in *Design of Computer Data Files*[1].

Plotting the average number of active records per block allows the user to apply the figures for his own case without being concerned about the total number of records in a block. For convenience, Table 4.1 includes the

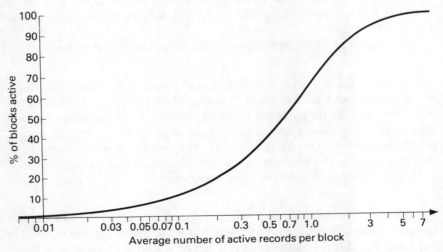

Fig. 4.3 This graph illustrates that as the blocking factor increases more unwanted data has to be read.

Table 4.1 These figures are calculated on the assumption that accesses are randomly distributed.

Blocking factor	Average number of active records per block	Percentage of records that must be read
1	0.01	1
3	0.03	3
10	0.10	9.5
30	0.30	26
100	1.0	63.2
300	3.0	95
1000	10.0	100

average number of active records per block for the example given there, and the reader can check that the figures lie on the curve. It is based on a random distribution of updates and should only be used when this can be assumed and the number of blocks in the file is large. It is clear from the curve that, as the blocking factor increases, more unwanted data has to be read.

A skip-sequential method of processing requires low blocking factors, to avoid reading unwanted data. Direct processing also can benefit from small blocks. Generally, however, larger blocks will improve performance by increasing the effective data transfer rate. Apart from the cases given above, the main reason for using small blocks is lack of space in main storage. When this is limited, the file designer may have to decide between the needs of several files. As a rule the more records in a file, the more advantage is gained by blocking. When there are only two or three files concerned, appropriate blocking factors can be calculated as follows:

For magnetic tape files, all the data has to be read, and only the total number of inter-block gaps in the files can be reduced. A run might handle three files, all of which are to be double buffered, with 5000 positions of main storage available for I/O areas.

File 1 (master)	100 000 records	250 characters per record
File 2 (ledger)	30 000 records	300 characters per record
File 3 (transactions)	30 000 records	25 characters per record

If all three files are held on magnetic tape with a transfer rate of 100 000 characters per second, and the start–stop time is 10 ms, tape passing time will be 347.5 s. The total number of start–stop times depends on blocking factors. By selecting a block size of ten records for File 3, its contribution is cut to 30 s; it can be virtually ignored from then on, although a more rigorous calculation would include varying this blocking factor also.

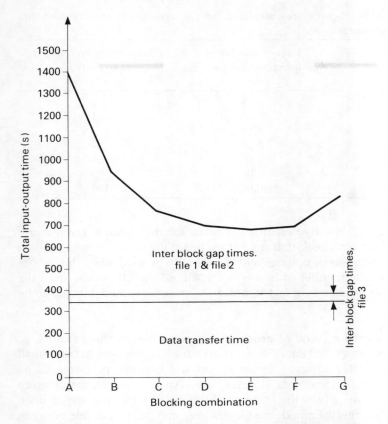

Fig. 4.4 This shows the contributions of record reading and start–stop times. The combination of File 1 records blocked in fives, and File 2 in threes, reduces total time to a minimum.

Table 4.2 gives the possible combinations of block size for Files 1 and 2, and the total times resulting from them. Figure 4.4 shows the contributions of record reading and start–stop times, which indicates that the combination of File 1 records blocked in fives and File 2 in threes, reduces total time to a minimum. In fact, the optimum solution is to block File 3 in fourteens, with File 1 in fives and File 2 in threes. This cuts the number of start–stop times to 32 143, and the total time to 669.5 s.

The advantage of using blocks of only 250 characters for File 3 in the preliminary calculations is that this allows the maximum variation of block sizes for the other files. The blocking factor for File 3 can be optimized by using any spare space remaining when the best combination has been selected for Files 1 and 2. In practice, some of these times would be

Table 4.2 This shows the possible combinations of block sizes for Files 1 and 2, and the total times resulting from them.

	A	B	C	D	E	F	G
Blocking File 1	1	2	3	4	5	6	7
Blocking File 2	6	5	5	4	3	2	1
Blocking File 3	10	10	10	10	10	10	10
Total CPU space required	4 600	4 500	5 000	4 900	4 800	4 700	4 600
Inter-block gaps							
File 1	100 000	50 000	33 334	25 000	20 000	16 667	14 286
File 2	5 000	6 000	6 000	7 500	10 000	15 000	30 000
File 3	3 000	3 000	3 000	3 000	3 000	3 000	3 000
Total	108 000	59 000	42 334	35 500	33 000	34 667	47 286
Time: IBG (s)	1 080	590	423	355	330	347	473
data (s)	348	348	348	348	348	348	348
Total time (s)	1 428	938	771	703	678	695	821

overlapped; it is still desirable to minimize them, particularly if the run is I/O bound.

In a complicated run situation, a more rigorous procedure is required, and the treatment is given on pp. 43–5. The same considerations apply to sequential disk file processing, but the position is more complex.

Conclusion

Record format can be used to improve the performance of data files. Although some installations decide on record size, blocking factor and other important design decisions without considering file performance, that is a mistake. At an early stage in the design cycle, the format of the records making up a file should be analyzed with a view to achieving the best possible file performance.

Revision questions

1 What is the total time required to process a given record? Set out the components of this time, and give an estimate of what they might be.

2 What is a balanced run? When would you try to achieve a balanced run? When and why would you not attempt to do so?

3 What should be optimized in handling a multiprogramming system?

4 What impact does record length have on file design?

5 Set out the advantages and disadvantages of fixed length records by comparison with variable length records.

6 If variable length records are decided on, what format would you advise?

7 How can record format affect record processing time?

8 Why are records blocked? Give figures to illustrate your answer.

9 What are the costs of blocking records? When are they important?

10 When different programs that use the same file have different space available for I/O areas, what space should you choose when calculating optimum blocking factors? Why?

11 How can you decide on optimum blocking factors for the files used by a particular program?

12 A tape run uses the following files:

File A (input)	50 000 records	210 characters per record
File B (output)	50 000 records	240 characters per record
File C (update)	3000 records	50 characters per record

All files are held on the same type of tape. 6000 characters are available for I/O areas. Calculate optimum blocking factors if files are double buffered.

13 In the above case, calculate the optimum blocking factors if the file specifications were as follows:

File A	75 000 records	195 characters per record
File B	50 000 records	305 characters per record
File C	10 000 records	25 characters per record

14 Calculate both the run times and the optimum integer blocking factors for files as follows:

File 1 100 000 records of 350 characters
File 2   50 000 records of 500 characters
File 3   50 000 records of 30 characters

All files are single buffered. 4000 storage positions are available. The tapes transfer 150 000 characters per second, and the inter-block gap time is 8 ms.

5 Sequential file design

Introduction

By the term **sequential files** we mean that the records in such a file are organized in a meaningful key order, usually ascending. To avoid confusion, it should be pointed out that **serial files** contain records in their order of arrival, and that their key sequence is not in any particular order. For example, the input to a sort program is serial, while the output is sequential.

A great deal of processing is carried out using sequential files, even in these days of enquiry systems and databases. The reasons are:

1. Many files require every record to be processed on each run. This applies to all update files and is usually true of master files such as payroll, for instance. These high hit-rate files are more efficiently processed sequentially than in any other way.
2. It is cheaper and easier to ensure the integrity of data from unintentional loss or damage if the processing mode is sequential, rather than any of the other file design techniques.
3. For most purposes a sequential report is very useful, as humans can easily reference information in such a report directly. Thus, when there is no particular need for an enquiry facility and the record hit-rate is high, the file designer will think first of sequential organization.
4. Files are processed sequentially to save time in locating records. It would be possible to handle all files in a random fashion, but this would usually be very wasteful. If a master file is held in a given key sequence, and input is batched and sorted into the same order, the time wasted in locating records for updating is minimized. If update data arrives by post, or as a result of a visit by a salesman or meter reader, it arises in a naturally batched form, making sequential processing even more logical.

When updates occur in real time, e.g. bookings by telephone, batching involves holding up the first to arrive until a batch has been built up. In this case, the service for earlier arrivals may be significantly worse than that for later ones, and this may lead to the use of a different file organization technique such as indexed sequential, to avoid delays.

The total time before output from a sequential run is available will be the sum of the following:

batching wait time (as the batch is built up)
+ *set up* (mounting tapes, initiating programs, etc.)
+ *sort* (sort batch of updates to master order)
+ *run* (match update and master records)
+ *output distribution*

This is shown in Fig. 5.1. The next record in a sequential magnetic tape file is available after a wait of only about 10 ms, and something like 10–25 ms on a sequential disk file. This compares with random seek times of about one minute on a magnetic tape, and 100–200 ms on a disk.

These figures make it clear that sequential processing can handle more records in a given time than direct (i.e. random) processing. Batching and sorting times will reduce this advantage, but unless the number of updates is very small, or the response required is very rapid, sequential processing of batched input will be more efficient than random processing. The break-even point for any given case can be estimated, as shown on p. 90.

Choice of file organization was discussed in Chapter 3. Once it is clear that a sequential file is required, the designer has a choice of storage media. The most usual situation is that tape or disk is available. Sometimes a compromise system such as IBM's 3850 mass-storage facility will be used, but this is in effect a direct access device so far as the user is concerned.

The choice is generally magnetic tape. This is because, for high hit-rates, magnetic tapes are usually more efficient; also tapes are cheaper—and likely to remain so now that fixed disks are widely used both on microcomputers and mainframes (the IBM 3350 is an example). These Winchester technology disks are usable in poor environmental conditions, but they are more expensive than earlier disks and have re-emphasized the price differential between the two media; even the very high capacity of 3370 and 3380 disks does not change this.

Sequential files on magnetic tapes

In magnetic tape handling of sequential files, every record has to be read. Any savings that are possible come from two sources: the first is correct blocking, and the second is hit-rate. If most records are updated already, hit-rate is not helpful. Often hit-rate is low, and it is possible to batch or section the file in such a way as to increase the hit-rate in the whole file, or some part of it.

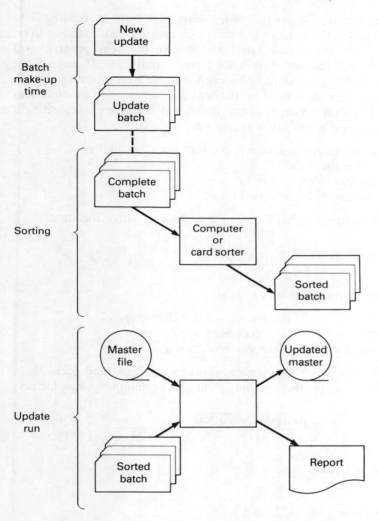

Fig. 5.1 Preparing for a sequential update run. Sorting may be carried out off-line using a card sorter, or on-line using the computer, in which case output would probably be onto magnetic tape.

Blocking

The general method of calculating optimum blocking factors is given here. Although the equations look formidable, readers equipped with a calculator will find that they do not take long to solve for any given set of files. As an example, we shall re-examine the case we looked at on p. 37.

In reading several files, a program cannot save time on reading data records. However, the number of inter-block gaps (IBGs) that have to be read depends on the blocking factors for each file. The program will only have a limited amount of space for input–output areas. If only *one* file were in use, its records would be blocked into the largest possible blocks and so reduce the time wasted by IBGs to a minimum. For multiple files Waters[3] and Walker[2] independently developed equations to calculate a minimum *total* number of IBGs taking into account:

S = main storage space available for I/O areas for all files
C_i = record length in file i
R_i = the number of records in file i
D_i = the number of buffers used for file i

The general equation is that the optimum blocking factor for file i

$$B_i = S \sqrt{R_i/C_i D_i} \Big/ \sum_{i=1}^{n} \sqrt{R_i C_i D_i}$$

Applying this to the previous example:

Master file   100 000 records of 250 characters
Ledger file   30 000 records of 300 characters
Transactions file   30 000 records of 25 characters

If the program has 5000 storage positions available and each file is double buffered, we get the following results for optimum blocking factors:

$$\sum_{i=1}^{3} \sqrt{R_i C_i D_i} = \sqrt{100\,000 \times 250 \times 2} + \sqrt{30\,000 \times 300 \times 2} + \sqrt{30\,000 \times 25 \times 2} = 12\,538.5$$

$$B_1 = 5000(100\,000/500)^{\frac{1}{2}}/12\,538.5$$
$$= 5.64$$

$$B_2 = 5000(30\,000/600)^{\frac{1}{2}}/12\,538.5$$
$$= 2.82$$

$$B_3 = 5000(30\,000/50)^{\frac{1}{2}}/12\,538.5$$
$$= 9.77$$

On a calculator this can be handled as follows:

1. Calculate $\qquad\qquad \sum_{i=1}^{n} \sqrt{R_i C_i D_i}$

2. Divide by $S \qquad\qquad \left(\sum_{i=1}^{n} \sqrt{R_i C_i D_i}/S \right)$

3. Invert (i.e. use $1/x$) $(S/\Sigma\sqrt{R_i\,C_i\,D_i})$

4. Store result

5. Calculate $R_i/C_i\,D_i$

6. Take square root $(\sqrt{R_i/C_i\,D_i})$

7. Multiply by the stored result. This gives B_i directly, and can be programmed on many calculators, to provide an 'optimum' result.

If it were possible to block records into fractional parts, this solution would be optimal, and would reduce the number of IBGs due to the three files to 31 440.

As fractions of a record are not feasible, Waters suggested truncation, which in this case would lead to a figure of 38 334 IBGs. Edwards[5] showed that truncation could lead to serious errors in some cases, and suggested the use of a program to search for the optimal *integer* (i.e. possible) solution.

The optimum in this case is to block File 1 in fives, File 2 in threes and File 3 in thirteens; generally, the best possible arrangement can be calculated quite quickly using the theoretical optimum as a starting point. In this case, extra space is given to File 2, as the figure of 2.82 is near 3. This means that 5.64 has to be reduced to 5, and the space remaining is allocated to File 3, giving a figure of 13.

Hit-rate

If this is already at or near 100 per cent, no further improvement is possible. If it is not, the designer will look for ways of increasing it.

1. If update runs are made less frequent, batches of updates will become larger and a greater proportion of master file records will be hit. This is 'efficient' in the file processing sense, but may be unacceptable to the user because of the longer wait for results. If this is the case a possible solution is to look at the pattern of updates.
2. Analysis of update pattern. If the pattern of updates is either random or unpredictable, no further improvement is possible. However, often updates are naturally bunched-meter readings in a single street, sales in an area that has been canvassed, etc.

In case (2), the designer's aim is to separate the **inactive sections** of the file from the **active**. The active element is separated, updated and recombined with a considerable saving in total run time. To take an example, a public utility file might be updated as shown in Fig. 5.2. If customers are billed quarterly, meter readers will read a thirteenth of the customers' meters each week. Appropriate customer numbers can ensure

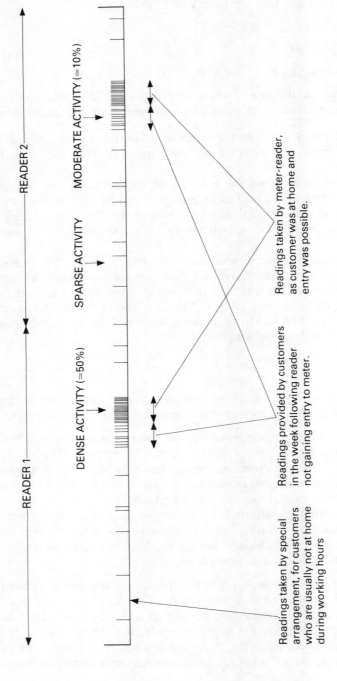

Fig. 5.2 A diagram showing the activity distribution within a file that is updated by a number of meter-readers on a 13-week cycle.

that these records are held in a group which represents about one thirteenth of the file.

In any given week, the meters that have been read will provide a high density of updates in the corresponding group of records. The previous group will yield a fair number of updates read by customers, as the meter reader could not gain entry when he called. The rest of the file will have only a few updates, representing readings by appointment at convenient times.

The designer could arrange for daily updates of the whole file. This would lead to an I/O bound run for much of the file, and (probably) a process-bound run while updating the current group. An alternative is to update the current group every day, but to update the whole file only once a week. At the same time, this week's 'current' group would be recombined with the main file, and next week's would be extracted.

This method of processing is illustrated in Fig. 5.3. It has the double advantage of cutting tape passing time, while increasing the activity of the non-current parts of the file, so improving the balance of the run between I/O and processing. An example of this method might be as follows.

A company has 1 300 000 customer records, each of 200 characters; 100 000 customers are billed each week. The file is held on magnetic tape with the following characteristics: transfer rate 160 kc/s; inter-block gap 0.6 in; start–stop time 5 ms; recording density 1600 characters/in; records blocked in 25 s.

The main file will take up 52 000 blocks. It will require

$$\left\{ \frac{1\ 300\ 000 \times 200}{1600} + 52\ 000 \times 0.6 \right\}$$

inches of tape, or 16 142 ft. This will mean that the file will he held on seven 2400 ft reels of tape. If the whole file is processed every day, tape passing time will be

$$5 \times \left\{ \frac{1\ 300\ 000 \times 200}{160\ 000} + 52\ 000 \times 0.005 \right\}$$

seconds, or 2 h 37 min a week. There will also be considerable tape handling time as seven reels have to be mounted during the run.

If the current part of the file is updated on the first four days, and the main file only on the fifth, tape passing time will be

$$4 \times (100\ 000 \times 200/160\ 000 + 4000 \times 0.005) + (2\ h\ 37\ min)/5$$
$$= 41\ min\ 5s\ per\ week$$

Sectioning a file of this size saves almost two hours of tape passing time a week, plus a great deal of reel handling time. When a sequential tape run is input–output bound, sectioning should always be considered.

Sometimes the techniques described here cannot be used, or do not lead to significant improvements. In this case, the designer should look at the possibility of improving file performance by holding the data on a direct-access device.

Sequential files on direct-access devices

There are a number of reasons why the file designer may decide not to hold a sequential file on magnetic tape. These include: low hit-rates, small files, some direct-access requirement, frequently sorted files, very high transfer rate and a requirement for very low error rates.

The first of these we shall look at in detail in the next section. The rest depend on inherent advantages provided by direct-access devices, and will be examined here.

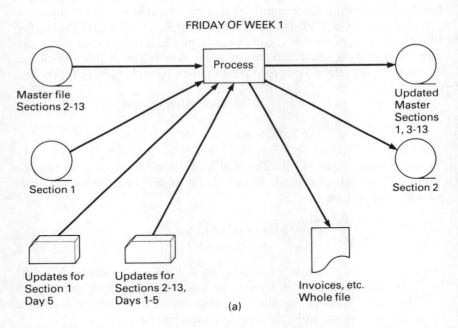

Fig. 5.3 Updating a sectioned file. The active section of the file is processed daily, and a new active section is selected weekly. This corresponds to a 13-week cycle with daily updates available, but this technique can be used for any time period and any number of sections. (a) The process on Friday of Week 1: Section 1 is recombined with the main file, while Section 2 is selected out. (b) Processing during Week 2.

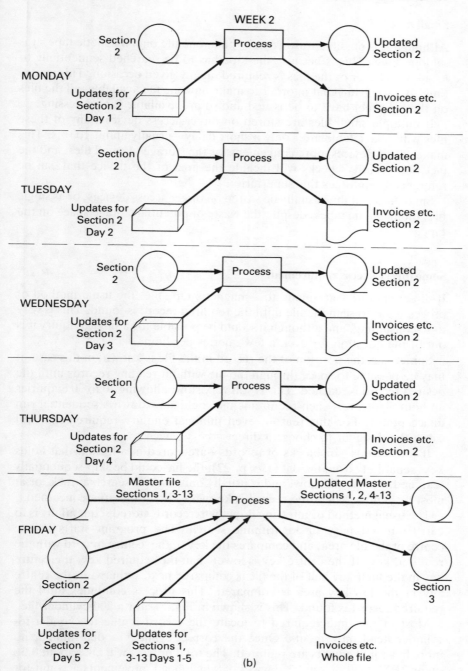

(b)

Small files

Although it is possible to store more than one file on a magnetic tape, it is seldom done. This is because the tape has to be searched sequentially to locate whichever of the files is required on any given occasion. This wastes time. It also means that in order to make any one file available, all the files on the tape reel have to be issued and so are available for processing.

If multiple small files are stored on direct-access devices, any of these files will be available after only a short delay—usually about 100 ms. This makes these devices more convenient for the storage of small files, and the fact that security checks will include the area of the device that can be referenced reinforces this superiority.

Small files will thus usually be stored on direct access devices, or as single files on magnetic tapes, despite the waste of potential storage space on the tape.

Some direct-access requirement

If direct enquiries are made to a magnetic tape file, the usual method of processing is to scan the file until the required record is found. This is very time-consuming, and although it would be possible for a single enquiry it is out of the question for even a few queries per hour.

Sometimes the position of the record in the file is known; in this case, it may be possible to space through the file without reading records until the desired record is reached. This is still very slow, allowing 20 to 30 enquiries an hour. However, such requirements would slow down a sequential run unacceptably. For this reason, even minimal enquiry requirements will cause the designer to choose a direct access device.

If the records—or blocks of records—are stored in a format that holds keys separately from the data (*see* p. 22), the file could be skip-sequentially searched. This is still slow, and is usually only used to search a track, or at most a cylinder, when the record is known to be in the area concerned.

The usual method of referring directly to records stored sequentially is to carry out a binary or logarithmic search. The program starts at the centre of the file area, and compares the key of the 'centre' record with the required key. If the centre key is lower than the required key, the centre key in the high-key half of the file is compared next. Otherwise, the centre key in the low-key area is compared. This process continues until the required record is found. This is shown in Fig. 5.4 for a 200-cylinder file.

Most of the time required to locate the record is due to cylinder-to-cylinder head movements. Once the correct cylinder is determined, no more head movements are required. The total process will take about 0.3 s on an IBM 3330 or similar device, of which head movements account for about three-quarters.

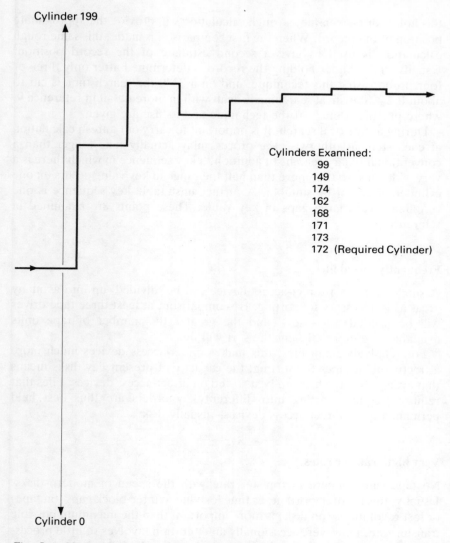

Cylinder 199

Cylinder 0

Cylinders Examined:
99
149
174
162
168
171
173
172 (Required Cylinder)

Fig. 5.4 Note that, although the third probe was within two of the required cylinder, it was not located until probe eight. Statistical binary searching usually avoids this waste of time.

In the case shown in Fig. 5.4, the third head movement was to cylinder 174. However, because of the binary search pattern, it required five more head movements before the required cylinder was determined. This is a weakness of the binary chop technique, and it can be considerably improved by using a statistical search.

Record keys are often fairly randomly distributed in a key sequence. If this holds for a given file, a rough calculation will provide the approximate position of the record. When the first comparison is made, this same rough calculation is used to give a second estimate of the record position. Usually, the cylinder holding the record is determined after only three or four probes using this technique, and on a 3330 the search time is cut to about 0.2 s. Statistical searching is dealt with in more detail in reference 9, where practical details of the technique and its use are given.

During a statistical search, it is important to carry out a fresh calculation at each step, as otherwise the process may actually take longer than a conventional binary search. In addition, a key sequence in which there is a very wide bias, so that more than half the range in key value occurs on one cylinder, may not be suitable. A further unsuitable key sequence is one containing very large gaps in key value. These points are examined in reference 9.

Frequently sorted files

A single area on a direct-access device can be 'divided' up into as many areas as is necessary for sorting. By comparison, at least three tape drives will be needed for a sort, and the greater the number of tape units available, the more efficient the sort will be.

For relatively small files, this makes direct-access devices much more attractive than tapes for sorting; the capacity of present day disks means that even very large files are best sorted on direct-access devices. Files that require frequent sorting into different key orders are thus best held permanently on direct-access devices—usually disk.

Very high transfer rates

No tape can compare in transfer rate with the speed of modern disks. Usually, this is not important, as time lost due to inter-block gaps (on tape) or lost revolutions (on disk) is more important than the maximum possible transfer rate. However, occasionally an operation involves so little processing delay—clear or copy disk, for example—that the full potential of disk can be used. When the processing required by a program is minimal, the designer may be able to achieve very rapid runs based on this.

A spiral file intended to achieve very high transfer rates is described on p. 109. Such files are not flexible, and can seldom be justified unless it is known that a file will remain stable, both in content and processing requirements, over long periods. While the user may occasionally consider this type of file, each one is so dependent on its own precise processing times and record sizes that general guidance is not possible. However, on the occasions that they are used, these files can be very effective.

Very low error rates

The reliability of modern disks is so good that files for which a failure during the run is not acceptable will be stored on disk. Winchester technology disks such as the IBM 3340, in which the read–write heads are enclosed in the disk pack, are more reliable than removable disks, but the difference is not great. Security precautions in general are discussed in Chapter 12, and will not be enlarged on here.

Apart from these special cases, direct-access devices will only be considered for sequential file storage when the hit-rate is relatively low. In the next section we shall look at the question of how low hit-rates have to be, before it is worth holding the file on a direct-access device on the basis of hit-rate alone.

Sequential files—tape or disk?

In previous sections, we have looked at the cases for which magnetic tape is the obvious choice, or disk is clearly indicated. The file designer is in a more difficult position when hit-rate is relatively low, but high enough to leave some doubt.

Estimating timings on magnetic tape does not present much difficulty. Every record has to be read, and savings can be made only by correct blocking, changes in batching or file sectioning. These were dealt with earlier.

Estimating timings on disk is more complicated. Generally, it is only if the separate key format is available that sequential disk files will be faster than sequential tape. The reason is that if the sector mode of operation is used, an indexed file will be needed to provide skip-sequential processing, in which unwanted records are scanned and rejected as the disk rotates. As the examination of every record will lead to the loss of many revolutions of the disk, only very low hit rates—perhaps 2–5 per cent of all blocks—will justify a sequential file being stored on sector-organized disks.

The rest of this discussion concentrates on comparing tapes with disks for which the separate key format is available.

On a disk, timing will depend on a number of factors. The first of these is a combination of hit-rate and blocking factor. This was discussed on pp. 36–7. It is clear that, as the size of blocks increases, more and more of the records have to be read whether they are required or not.

The next important influence on timing is the type of access. This is shown in Table 5.1.

Loss of full revolutions will lead to very much slower processing than is required to access records for a single read or write; hence, the balance of decision between disk and tape will depend very much on the type of processing required.

Table 5.1 The unavoidable delay in handling records due to the type of access required. Software may impose a further delay in addition.

Access type	Delay
READ or WRITE only	No automatic delay

READ followed by WRITE
    WRITE followed by CHECK
	At least *one* lost revolution per
	    record processed

READ followed by WRITE
    followed by CHECK
	At least *two* lost revolutions per
	    record processed

For any given installation, the characteristics of the disks and tapes available will determine break-even points. These will be affected by the operation of the manufacturers' software, and this is sometimes decisive. ICL 1900 series sequential files on disk could only read one record on a single track revolution, for example[24]. However, software can be modified by writing user routines in physical IOCS (PERI routines for the 1900 series, PIOCS for IBM computers), so it is still worth comparing the potential differences between tape and disk.

A tape of the following characteristics has been examined:

Rated transfer rate	150 000 bytes/s
Packing density	1600 bytes/in
Start–stop time	6.4 ms
Inter-block gap (IBG)	0.6 in

This tape will have effective transfer rates for a number of block sizes as shown in Table 5.2. The figures come from a paper by the author[8].

Table 5.2 The effect of block size on the effective transfer rate achieved between tape and main storage.

Block size (records)	Effective transfer rate (bytes/s)
1	60 000
2	85 700
3	102 100
4	108 000
8	126 300
16	137 000

It is useful to note how, for small blocks, the effective transfer rate is much lower than the rated one. This is reflected in Fig. 5.5, which shows—for a 50 per cent hit-rate—the relationship between block size, the processing time required for hit records and the average record run time for the complete file.

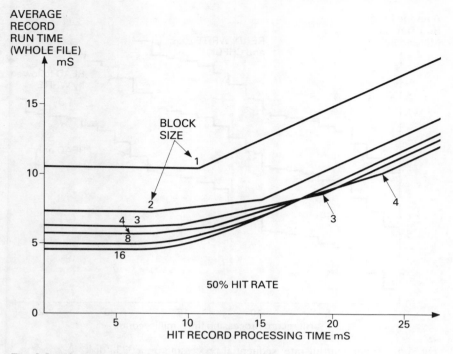

Fig. 5.5   50 per cent hit-rate; sequential processing on magnetic tape.

The shape of these curves demonstrates that small block sizes—one or two records in this case—never give as good results as larger blocks. However, for some rather long record processing times, intermediate sized blocks can outperform large ones. The arrowed points show where three and four record blocks give particularly good results.

This should not obscure the usual situation, which is that for typical record processing times, and for lower hit-rates, large blocks always provide the shortest average record processing time. Further details of this work are given in references 1, 8 and 10.

Manufacturers' software may not yield results precisely like these, and average record run times will generally be higher. However, the potential is there to be exploited, and the best that can be achieved is indicated by this sort of analysis.

As explained earlier, disk results depend on the mode of access required. The relationship between average record run time and hit record processing time is shown for the 50 per cent hit-rate case on a 3330 in Fig. 5.6. The characteristically 'stepped' curves are due to lost revolutions, and their derivation is given in references 8 and 10. Once more, the curves show a potential situation that is not realized by many of the available software packages. Average record run times are often much higher than

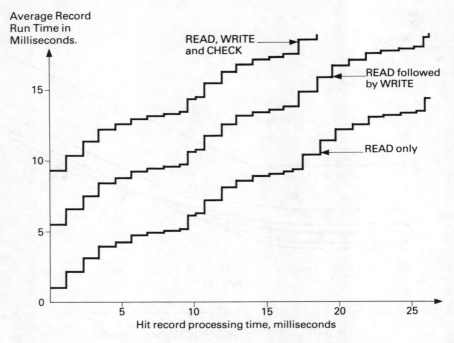

Average Record
Run Time in
Milliseconds.

Fig. 5.6 50 per cent hit-rate; sequential processing on a 3330 disk.

this, due to the loss of revolutions as a result of software written without taking into account the way disks operate.

Combining the data in Fig. 5.5 and 5.6 with many other curves for different block sizes and hit-rates, it is possible to produce curves such as those shown in Fig. 5.7. These represent the potential break-even points between disk and tape for the particular tape stated above, and IBM's 2311, 2314 and 3330 disks. These relatively slow drives have been chosen as their transfer rates start at about that of the tape.

As one would expect, a 2311 does not outperform this tape except when blocks are very small. The 2314 is superior over a wider range, and the 3330 for a substantial range of blocking factors and hit-rates. It must be emphasized that the two lines here represent the boundaries to areas in which disk is quicker for READ, PROCESS, WRITE and CHECK, and READ, PROCESS, WRITE.

The READ ONLY or WRITE ONLY case is more complicated, and not conveniently shown in a diagram. However, a 3330 is always faster than tape for short processing times and for hit-rates below 60 per cent. A 2311, by contrast, never outperforms blocks of four or more records on tape.

All of the above conclusions depend on the software being used. The only safe way to decide between disk and tape in a given installation is to

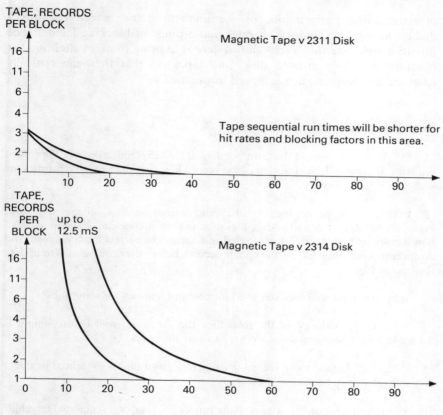

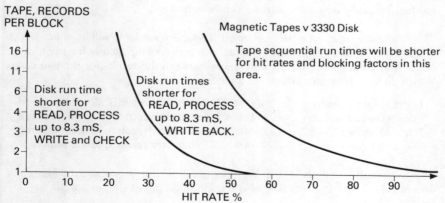

Fig. 5.7 (a) Magnetic tape v 2311 disk; (b) Magnetic tape v 2314 disk; (c) Magnetic tape v 3330 disk.

investigate the performance of the units available, which requires a dedicated machine, known hit-rates and a range of blocking factors. The intention in giving the graphs shown here is to bring to users attention the potential available in both disks and tapes, so that they can critically examine the performance achieved in practice.

Revision questions

1 Define the meaning of the term 'sequential file', explaining the way the record sequence is arranged, the position of the record key, and the available formats for such files.

2 Compare the processing of serial and sequential files, giving your own examples of the master and update files used in each update run. Explain in detail how a given update record is used to find and update the correct master record, and any preprocessing needed for the update records before they can be used to update the master file.

3 Why are sequential files still used in most installations for some jobs?

4 What is the make-up of the total time the user must wait before output is available from a sequential run? What can you alter—and how?

5 Which can handle more record updates in a given time—sequential or direct processing? Justify your answer carefully.

6 Where can we look for savings in the processing time of a sequential tape file? Explain generally how these savings can be achieved.

7 A four-file tape run is being planned. The space available will be either 10 000 or 35 000 characters. Calculate optimum integer blocking factors for the files set out below, commenting on the differences between the results for the two cases. Which do you think more likely on a modern machine?

File 1 (Input master)	250 000 × 325 character records, double buffered
File 2 (Output master)	225 000 × 325 character records, double buffered
File 3 (Journal)	525 000 × 310 character records, double buffered
File 4 (Update)	50 000 × 35 character records, single buffered

8 Repeat the analysis in the previous question, for a program handling five files in (a) 5 k, (b) 25 k, (c) 50 k of space for all the input–output areas.

File 1 (Input master)	75 000 × 675 character records, double buffered
File 2 (Output master)	90 000 × 675 character records, double buffered
File 3 (Update)	25 000 × 75 character records, single buffered
File 4 (Journal)	175 000 × 60 character records, single buffered
File 5 (Print file)	10 000 × 160 character records, single buffered

9 In the daily update of a gas customer invoice file, the invoicing program selects out a number of accounts, because they do not lie within 50 per cent of the expected figure. All other invoices are processed normally. The program has 14 500 character-storage positions available for input–output areas. The tapes in use transfer data at 1 250 000 characters/s, with an inter-block time of 3 ms. All tapes are attached to the same channel. Calculate optimum integer blocking factors for the files below, and suggest ways of reducing the total run time. What happens if files are single buffered?

File 1 (Input)	1 313 000 × 480 character records, double buffered
File 2 (Output)	1 313 000 × 480 character records, double buffered
File 3 (Update)	20 200 × 30 character records, double buffered
File 4 (Print)	20 000 × 500 character records, double buffered
File 5 (Exception)	200 × 525 character records, double buffered

10 Why is the calculated optimum blocking factor not generally usable?

11 Describe and explain the principle of sectioning a file.

12 When might the designer choose to use a direct access device to hold a sequentially organized file?

13 Explain the principle of skip-sequential searching, logarithmic searching and statistical searching of a sequential disk file. What precautions should you take in setting up a statistical search?

14 Compare the process of referring to records on disk or tape, with particular reference to the elements of timing, and the reference required.

15 Explain the general considerations involved in a decision between disk or tape as the storage medium for a sequential file; assume that the hit-rate is around 10 per cent, which you believe to be relatively low.

16 How might the software you are using affect the decision in question 15?

17 You have a master file on tape, and each record contains a name, an address and an age. Explain how you would (a) update the file with new records, (b) obtain a list in alphabetical order, (c) provide a list of names for agents in each of the 27 towns covered by the file, (d) prepare a listing in ascending age order for a friend who sells insurance. Give all run diagrams, explain every operation on the file, and comment on how suitable this organization was for the jobs in question.

6 Direct file design

Introduction

Sequentially organized files on disk can handle occasional enquiries using either a binary or statistically-based search technique, as described on pp. 50–2. The total number of enquiries that can be handled in this way is very limited, however, as it will take 200–400 ms just to locate the required record, without considering processing time. Reference times can be cut to about a fifth of this figure by using a well-designed direct file.

Addressing concepts

The term **direct** implies that, when a particular record is required, it is possible to retrieve it without scanning a large part of the file during the search. This means that the record **key**—which will be known from the enquiry—is related in some way to the record **address**, which is required to retrieve it.

Self-indexing files

The simplest way to arrange for this relationship is to store records in addresses that are directly linked to their keys, for example:

ADDRESS = KEY
ADDRESS = KEY + CONSTANT
ADDRESS = (KEY + CONSTANT)/BLOCKING FACTOR

There are many variations of this type of equation, due to factors such as differing disk starting addresses, blocking of records or form of keys. They all rely on one essential prerequisite, which is that the key sequence is unbroken, or at least nearly so.

Because a simple relationship provides an **unique address** for each record or block of records, the user may wish to preserve it even if this means that some addresses are unoccupied. A file stored in this way is called **self-indexing**.

Even if the key sequence was originally unbroken, gaps occur naturally when stock lines are discontinued, customers go out of business or employees leave. Preservation of the relationship by leaving up to half the potential storage space unoccupied may be justified; the file designer will be guided by the availability of disk storage and the importance of maximum enquiry throughput. At some point, it will not be possible to waste more storage space as the key sequence deteriorates, and a different solution has to be found.

If the gaps are large but relatively few in number, a table can be provided that will subtract appropriate values from the keys, and allow all addresses to be used. In a simple case, the keys might follow the sequence

$$0001 \longrightarrow 0103$$
$$0121 \longrightarrow 0244$$
$$0443 \longrightarrow 0480$$
$$\text{etc.}$$

If addresses were available from disk sector 000870, and each sector could hold a single record, the address of a record would be determined as follows:

$$\text{IF} \qquad\qquad \text{KEY} \leq 103, \quad \text{ADDRESS} = \text{KEY} + 869$$
$$\text{IF} \quad 121 \leq \text{KEY} \leq 224, \quad \text{ADDRESS} = \text{KEY} + 852$$
$$\text{IF} \quad 443 \leq \text{KEY} \leq 480, \quad \text{ADDRESS} = \text{KEY} + 634$$

and so on.

Such an allocation arrangement is very useful for cases in which runs of keys occur naturally—*see* reference 1 for details. However, it involves both the provision of comparison values, and a lengthy analysis of each input key. In principle, it could always be arranged, but in practice the technique is limited by availability of storage space or the need to take account of constant changes in key sequence. Thus it is only useful if the file is relatively stable and gaps in the key sequence are few—that is, hundreds at the most.

Whenever it is possible to link the address and key of a record directly and so provide a self-indexing file, both direct and sequential reference are possible without any waste of time. However, some key sequences have too many gaps to be handled in this way, or are unsuitable because they contain alphabetic or special characters. In this case, some other method of linking the key and address is needed.

Algorithmic addressing

Keys may have values that span a very wide range, and the objective is to fit them into a set of addresses that provides enough space for all the records, without very many empty positions (10–20 per cent of empty spaces is usually acceptable). The process is shown in Fig. 6.1. Two approaches to this are possible. The first is to spread the records over the

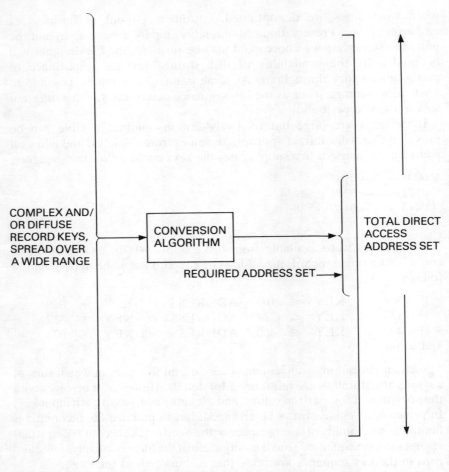

Fig. 6.1 The process of reduction of the range of values in a diffuse key sequence to fit the available addresses.

available addresses *at random*. The second is to use any order in the key sequence—usually groups or runs of keys—to allocate them more effectively. The allocation calculation is called an **algorithm**. Many types of algorithm have been investigated— *see* references 11, 12, 13, 14, 15. We shall only look at the two most useful techniques here, as the others are seldom used. Further details are given in *Design of Computer Data Files*[1].

Truly random allocation of records is often achieved by squaring the key, or a part of it, and using some digits from the square (usually the centre digits) as an address. The figure will usually have to be adjusted in some way, as it will have a range of 2^n or 10^n, while the required address range might be of any size, depending on the number of records in the file.

Kaimann[14] showed that the results of using this technique come very close to those calculated on the assumption of absolutely random allocation.

Use of this technique will lead to more than one record being allocated to some addresses and none at all to others. The first record can be stored in its expected address, and is called a **home record**. If addresses can only hold a single record, second and subsequent records allocated to this address will have to be stored elsewhere. They are called **synonyms**. The occurrence of synonyms is often said to be due to **collisions**.

It is virtually impossible to find an algorithm that does not produce synonyms. Heising[18] quotes the probability of finding such an algorithm in allocating 4000 records to 5000 addresses as 1 in $10^{12\,000}$. However, sometimes the order in the keys (usually runs of keys differing by 1, i.e. n, $n+1, n+2 \ldots$) allows us to reduce the number of synonyms below the percentages that would be predicted if records are allocated completely randomly.

Division of the key by a prime number, or an odd number not too close to 10^n (e.g. not 99 997, 100 001), and use of the remainder as an address, will often give a very good distribution of records. This is discussed in detail in reference 12. The advantage of this method is that runs of keys will produce remainders that do not lead to synonyms, as they differ by 1 from each other. However, if two separate runs overlap, large numbers of synonyms can be caused. This will be discussed later.

Division also allows the number of addresses allocated to be 'fitted' easily to the number of records by a suitable choice of divisor; division by N will produce N remainders in the range $0 \longrightarrow (N-1)$, and the only further adjustment needed is to add a constant if the available space on disk does not start at address 0.

These two techniques are widely used, and give good results. However, synonyms cause wasted time, as the initial address calculation leads only to the home address, and a further search is needed to find the required record. Thus the file designer aims to reduce both the *number* and the *effect* of synonyms to a minimum.

Minimizing the number of synonyms

Synonyms cause loss of time in locating records, as they are not at the expected address. It is therefore essential to reduce their numbers to a minimum. The factors the designer will consider in doing this are: choice of algorithm, bucket size, packing density and loading technique.

Choice of algorithm

A completely randomized set of keys gives a useful benchmark against which to compare the performance of any given algorithm. Figure 6.2

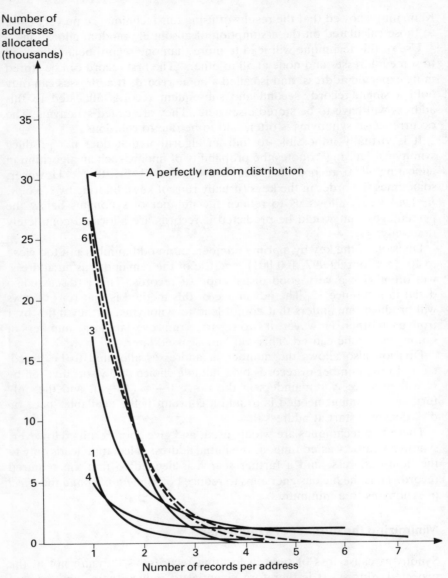

Number of
addresses
allocated
(thousands)

Fig. 6.2 The results of using a number of algorithms to randomize records to addresses compared with theoretically perfect randomization.

shows the results of experiments carried out by Kaimann[14] on a single large file. The line marked 5 was the result of a mid-square randomization, while that marked 6 was due to a division algorithm. Neither were as effective in producing home records as the 'theoretical' curve, and division in this case was not as good as mid-square. However, Lum, Yuen and Dodd[13] found division to be better than the theoretically calculated values for eight files they tested—at least in most circumstances. Their results are shown in Fig. 6.3. Thus it is advisable, for any given case, that the algorithm being considered should be compared with the theoretical prediction by running the keys against the algorithm, and calculating the resulting synonyms. If it is as good as or better than the predition, then it is acceptable. If it is significantly worse, a new algorithm should be tried.

Programs to carry out the comparison are available from many bureaux. A check on the expected numbers of synonyms can be made by using Table 6.1 and these figures are plotted in Fig. 6.4.

Once a satisfactory algorithm for this file has been chosen, the next factor will be examined.

Bucket size

An addressable area on direct-access storage is referred to as a bucket when direct files are discussed. A bucket may hold one or more records; if it holds multiple records, the term 'block' is not used, because this would suggest that the records are related in some logical way. In a direct file, the relation is that they randomize to the same address. The chance of more than one record from a bucket being required at the same time will be very low, so the relation between the records is not useful in the way that it is in a block of records arranged in sequential order.

Larger buckets would be expected to reduce the effect of 'local' variations, and the values given in Table 6.1 and Fig. 6.4 show that a large bucket does reduce the number of synonyms very markedly.

The problem with large buckets is that they will take up a large area in main storage and require significant transfer time, but yet provide only a single useful record. Montgomery[19] stated that a full track bucket is *never* justified, while Severance and Duhne[15] make a similar comment. This is true if all the records in the bucket have to be transferred into main storage just to retrieve one of them. However, if it is possible to *address* a large bucket—a full track, for instance—but *transfer* only the required record, then the benefits of large bucket size are combined with those of individual record retrieval.

This can be achieved if the separate key and data format is available (*see* p. 20 for details). Records have to be stored individually, as even blocks of two records held in a larger bucket would lead to the need to read the block to check the two keys in main storage. By comparison, the key of an individual record can be checked by the device itself, and only desired records need to be read into the CPU after keys have been matched.

Increased numbers of records per bucket will markedly reduce synonym

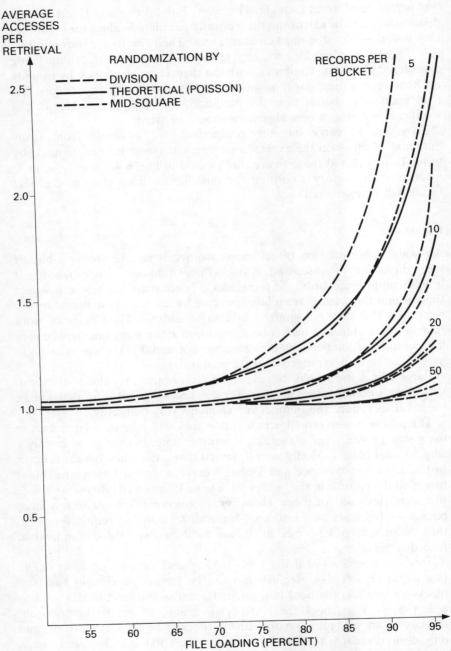

Fig. 6.3 A comparison of Lum *et al.*'s results for division and mid-square randomization with the theoretically predicted figures for several bucket sizes.

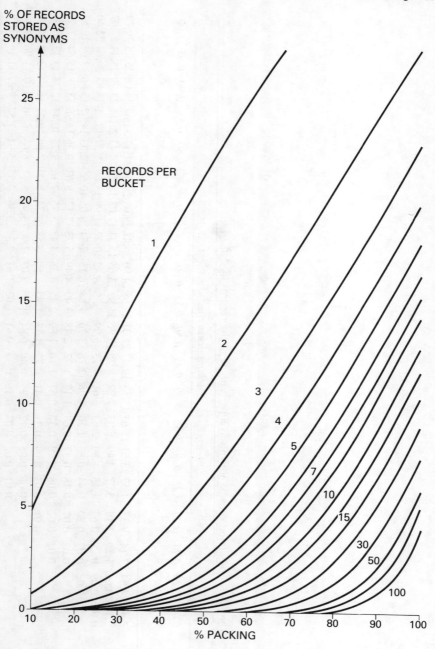

Fig. 6.4 The combined effect of bucket size and packing density on the theoretically predicted percentage of synonyms in a direct file.

Table 6.1 The figures tabulated show synonyms as a percentage of the records loaded.

Records per bucket	Packing density α																			
	0.05	0.10	0.15	0.20	0.25	0.30	0.35	0.40	0.45	0.50	0.55	0.60	0.65	0.70	0.75	0.80	0.85	0.90	0.95	1.00
1	2.46	4.84	7.14	9.37	11.52	13.61	15.63	17.58	19.47	21.31	23.08	24.80	26.47	28.08	29.65	31.17	32.64	34.06	35.45	36.79
2	0.16	0.60	1.29	2.19	3.27	4.49	5.83	7.27	8.78	10.36	11.99	13.65	15.34	17.03	18.73	20.43	22.11	23.79	25.44	27.07
3	0.01	0.09	0.29	0.63	1.13	1.80	2.63	3.61	4.73	5.99	7.35	8.82	10.37	11.99	13.66	15.37	17.11	18.87	20.64	22.40
4		0.02	0.07	0.20	0.44	0.80	1.30	1.96	2.78	3.76	4.88	6.15	7.54	9.05	10.65	12.33	14.07	15.86	17.69	19.54
5			0.02	0.07	0.18	0.37	0.68	1.12	1.72	2.48	3.40	4.49	5.73	7.12	8.63	10.26	11.98	13.78	15.64	17.55
6			0.01	0.02	0.08	0.18	0.37	0.67	1.10	1.69	2.45	3.38	4.48	5.75	7.18	8.75	10.44	12.24	14.12	16.06
7				0.01	0.03	0.09	0.21	0.41	0.72	1.18	1.80	2.60	3.58	4.74	6.09	7.60	9.25	11.04	12.93	14.90
8					0.02	0.05	0.12	0.25	0.49	0.84	1.35	2.03	2.90	3.97	5.23	6.68	8.30	10.07	11.96	13.96
9					0.01	0.02	0.07	0.16	0.33	0.61	1.02	1.61	2.38	3.36	4.55	5.94	7.52	9.27	11.16	13.18
10						0.01	0.04	0.10	0.23	0.44	0.79	1.29	1.98	2.88	3.99	4.80	6.86	8.59	10.48	12.51
11						0.01	0.02	0.07	0.16	0.33	0.61	1.04	1.66	2.48	3.53	4.36	6.30	8.01	9.90	11.94

	0.01	0.02	0.06	0.18	0.30	0.57	1.01	1.65	2.52	3.64	5.05	6.70	8.54	10.60
14	0.01	0.02	0.06	0.18	0.30	0.57	1.01	1.65	2.52	3.64	5.05	6.70	8.54	10.60
16	0.01	0.03	0.10	0.19	0.39	0.74	1.28	2.05	3.09	4.41	6.00	7.85	9.92	
18		0.02	0.06	0.12	0.28	0.55	1.01	1.70	2.65	3.90	5.45	7.28	9.36	
20		0.01	0.04	0.08	0.20	0.42	0.81	1.42	2.30	3.48	4.99	6.80	8.88	
25		0.01	0.03	0.09	0.22	0.48	0.93	1.65	2.70	4.10	5.86	7.95		
30			0.01	0.04	0.12	0.29	0.64	1.23	2.16	3.47	5.18	7.26		
35				0.02	0.06	0.18	0.45	0.94	1.76	2.98	4.64	6.73		
40			0.01	0.04	0.12	0.32	0.73	1.46	2.60	4.22	6.30			
50				0.01	0.05	0.17	0.46	1.04	2.05	3.57	5.63			
60				0.02	0.09	0.30	0.76	1.65	3.10	5.14				
75				0.01	0.04	0.16	0.50	1.25	2.59	4.60				
100					0.01	0.07	0.27	0.83	2.02	3.99				
150						0.01	0.09	0.43	1.37	3.26				
200							0.03	0.24	1.01	2.82				
250							0.01	0.14	0.78	2.52				
300							0.01	0.09	0.62	2.30				
400								0.04	0.42	1.99				
500								0.02	0.30	1.78				
600								0.01	0.22	1.63				

percentages. However, once synonyms begin to appear, addition of further records leads to a rapid increase in the number of synonyms in the file. This is associated with increasing record packing density, as can be seen in Fig. 6.4.

Packing density

Table 6.1 and Fig. 6.4 show that one way of reducing the number of synonyms in a file is to provide much more space than is required to hold the records. However, the effect is less marked than that of bucket size, and the designer will usually choose a combination of packing density and bucket size that meets design requirements rather than considering either factor in isolation.

It is seldom possible to allow a packing density of less than 50 per cent, and most files are designed to be 75–85 per cent packed when they are set up. Lower densities are usually only appropriate for very volatile files to which many additions can be expected.

A file that is changing in size or—even worse—varying in size within a wide range, presents a problem to the designer. Reorganization of the file is basically caused by the need to 'fit' it into a new file area, and this will mean that a new algorithm has to be selected and tested at frequent intervals.

A stable-sized file is ideal for direct handling; additions and deletions do not generally cause a problem, although cases where they can be damaging are discussed on pp. 73–4. So long as the overall number of active records remains the same, file performance should be predictable.

There is one further precaution that can be taken to minimize the number of synonyms. This is to avoid creating them by incorrect loading.

Loading technique

If records are loaded in a single pass, synonyms are stored at the same time as home records. This is called a **one-pass load**, and means that a synonym may take up a position that will later be required for a potential home record. As there is no longer space for this record, it too has to be stored as a synonym. The situation is shown in Fig. 6.5.

This can be avoided if the file is loaded in two passes. Only home records are loaded on the first pass, while synonyms are loaded on a second pass. This method is known as a **two-pass load**.

Some authors have recommended sorting the file into sequential order before loading, and reported reduced synonyms as a result. It is probable that this is due to the division method of randomization producing sets of non-clashing addresses from runs of keys. Sorting will ensure that all the

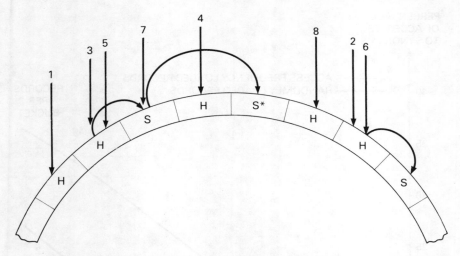

Fig. 6.5 If the second record that randomizes to a position is immediately stored (in S in this case), a later record that would have been a home record in that position has also to be stored as a synonym (S*). H represents home, S synonyms, S* an unnecessary synonym.

keys in a run are loaded together, so synonyms will not be caused due to other records breaking up the sequence.

When all the above precautions have been taken, the number of synonyms in the file should be at a minimum. A comprehensive discussion of this is given in reference 1, for readers who wish to explore it further. It only remains to minimize their effect.

Reducing the effect of synonyms

When the number of synonyms in a file has been minimized, we have to ensure that those remaining cause as little waste of time as possible. There are two ways of doing this:

loading the most-referenced records first;
ensuring that synonyms are quickly retrieved.

Let us look at these possibilities.

Access frequency loading

It is often stated that '90 per cent of accesses are to 10 per cent of records', or '80 per cent of accesses are to 20 per cent of records'—or some similar split.

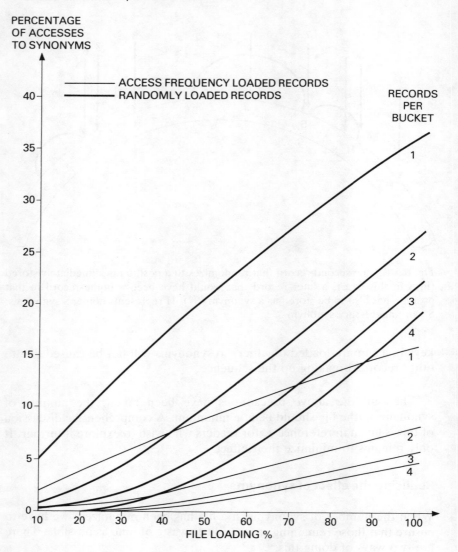

Fig. 6.6 The effect of access-frequency loading (the 80/20 case).

When this applies, there is clearly a benefit to be gained by loading the most-referenced records first.

The size of this benefit in the 80/20 case (the second quoted) can be judged from Fig. 6.6. An interesting point here is that the benefit *increases* with increasing bucket size up to about six records per bucket. An analysis of the improvement to be expected in any given case is presented in reference 21.

For the 80/20 case and bucket sizes of six or more, accesses to synonyms are reduced to one quarter of the figure recorded in the random case. When 90 per cent of the accesses are to 10 per cent of records, buckets of size five or more will show a reduction to one ninth of random access figures. In general, when A per cent of the accesses are to B per cent of the records, the maximum improvement possible[21] will be a reduction to A/B of the random access figures.

These results are dramatic, and allow 90–95 per cent packed files to give as good a performance as conventionally-loaded files of 70–75 per cent packing. The user will want to know: how to get these results; when it is not going to be possible to obtain them; any drawbacks involved.

Information required

Data on the frequency of accesses to the file has to be obtained; when a file is first set up, a 'guesstimate' is as much as can be expected, but data can then be collected during later runs in one of two ways.

If records are read and then written back, an additional single or double byte count field can be added to each record, set up as binary zeros and incremented each time the record is updated. After sufficient time has elapsed to give a large count in the most referenced records, the file is sorted into *descending* count field order and reloaded with the most-referenced records first. Counts may be recorded and rezeroed, or continue. Once it is clear that the access frequency pattern is reasonably stable, the count fields can be used for other purposes.

If the records are only being referenced and not written back, the above method would involve an additional rotational delay just to update the count field. In this case, it is better to use an ancillary file, consisting only of record keys and count fields, and probably organized in indexed-sequential form, to collect the data. Its small size ensures rapid access. Otherwise, the process is just as described above.

Unsuitable files

If a file is very variable in access pattern or if it has a short life, this sort of data is not obtainable. The designer will have to accept that the normal conditions of random access will apply.

File degradation

Additions to an access-frequency loaded file will generally be more active than the average, as they are new customers, products, etc. They will certainly be a random mix, and will include a proportion of very active records. This leads to rapid degradation of the file, the extent of which is shown in Fig. 6.7. The file will still require less accesses to synonyms than a conventionally loaded file, but the advantage grows less as more random additions are made.

Figures 6.8 and 6.9 show the accesses to synonyms as a result of normal loading, and 60/40, 70/30, 80/20, 90/10 and 99/5 case access-frequency loaded files for single- and ten-record buckets in the range 55–100 per cent packing. These are the continuous lines. The effects of random additions are shown as dashed lines, with the figures on the right showing the packing density from which *random* additions were made to the 90/10 case. One of these dashed lines, or lines similar to them, will be followed as a result of random additions regardless of the starting point, as they are a family of curves that do not overlap. This is examined in detail in reference 21.

Summing up, additions to and deletions from a direct file hardly alter the performance of conventionally loaded files, but badly degrade an access-frequency loaded file. The ideal file for this purpose has a static record set without additions or deletions, and is long-lived.

Overflow handling

The other area in which the performance of direct files can be improved is that of synonym storage. Three methods of handling synonyms are widely used; these are progressive overflow, chaining and tagging. The last two are shown in Fig. 6.10.

Progressive overflow

Synonyms can be stored in the next available position following their home bucket. This has the advantage that no complex links are required, but means that there is no indication a synonym exists. A reference to a record that is not in the file (for example, due to a non-existent key being used) would not be detected as an error until the whole file had been searched. This can be prevented by recording the longest search for a storage bucket during file creation or addition, and limiting searches during reference to this length.

In addition, if a home record is deleted, a synonym, if there is one, has to be located and put into the home position, otherwise it will appear that the address is free and no synonyms exist.

Chained records

In this case, the last home record is linked to the first synonym, the first synonym to the second and so on. Many writers recommend a separate overflow area for chained records, but it is better to store the records using

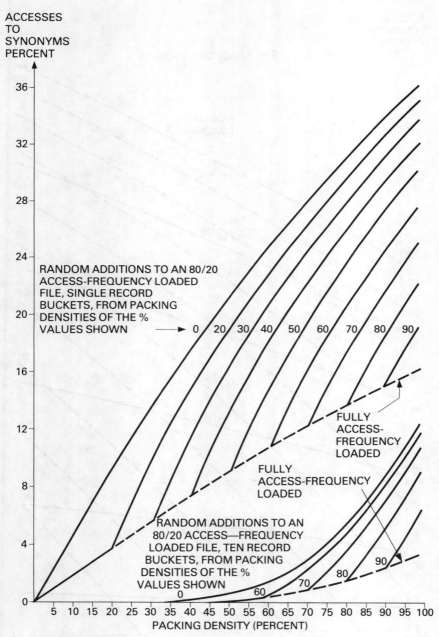

Fig. 6.7 The effect of bucket size on random additions to access-frequency loaded files. The dashed lines show the result of access-frequency loading up to 100 per cent.

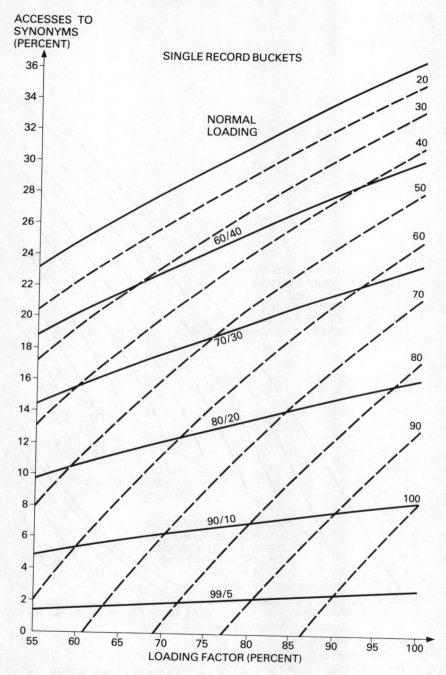

Fig. 6.8 Single-record buckets.

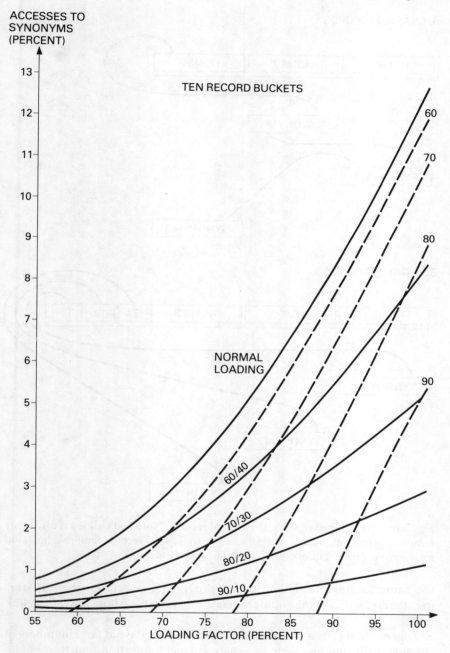

Fig. 6.9 Ten-record buckets.

A. CHAINED RECORDS

B. TAGGED RECORDS

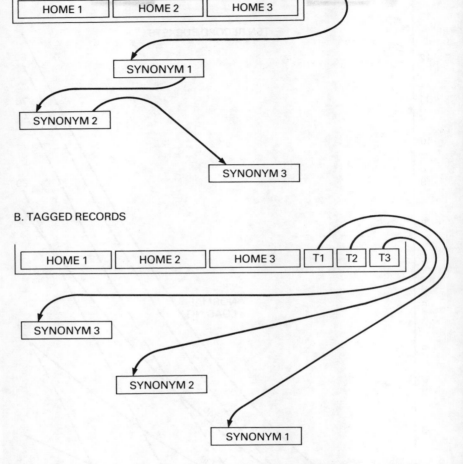

Fig. 6.10 (a) Chained records. (b) Tagged records. Note that chained records only require a *single* link field in the home address. Tagged records require a link field for *every* synonym, but avoid following a chain of records.

the same location technique as for progressive overflow—that is, storing them as near the home record as possible—but providing link fields.

This method puts a premium on algorithms that avoid large numbers of synonyms for any *one* address. There is some indication that true randomization performs better than division in this respect. Johnson[20] showed that ensuring the minimum length of chains by moving up synonyms into the

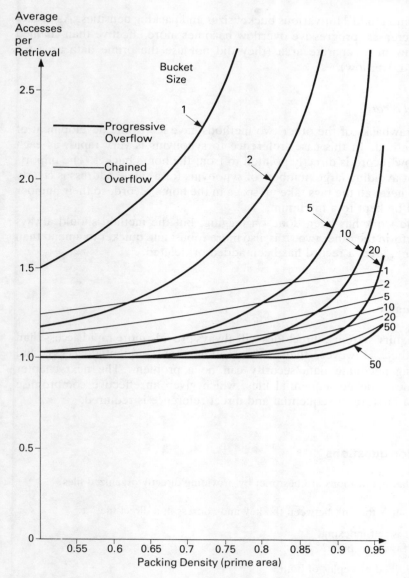

Average
Accesses
per
Retrieval

Bucket
Size

2.5 –

1

Progressive
Overflow

2

Chained
Overflow

2.0 –

5

10

20

1.5 –
1
2
5
10
20
50

1.0 –
50

0.5 –

0 –
0.55   0.6   0.65   0.7   0.75   0.8   0.85   0.9   0.95
Packing Density (prime area)

Fig. 6.11 Comparison of progressive overflow and chained overflow techniques.

home bucket markedly improved performance. However, so long as link fields are protected, additions and deletions do not present any particular difficulty.

Most reported work has been carried out as a comparison of chained overflow and progressive overflow. Figure 6.11 shows the results of Lum,

Yuen and Dodd[13] for various bucket sizes and packing densities. As bucket size increases, progressive overflow becomes more effective than chained overflow in a separate area (they did not use the prime data area for chained overflow).

Tagged records

The drawbacks of the other two methods have led to the development of this method. In this case, reference to synonyms is very rapid, as each overflow record is directly pointed to from the home bucket. The importance of avoiding large numbers of synonyms for a single address is clearly shown here; all the tags take up space in the home record, so their number should be kept to a minimum.

Little work has been done on tagging, but the method should always outperform the other two. It is also more robust and quicker to amend than chaining, after a record has been added or deleted.

Conclusion

For enquiry systems, direct files will always provide more rapid access than any other. However, they do not allow rapid sequential access, and ensuring adequate data security can be a problem. The next chapter examines indexed-sequential files, which given an effective compromise when a mixture of sequential and direct reference is required.

Revision questions

1 What applications are best met by providing directly organized files?

2 What is the link between the key and address in a direct file,

(a) if it is self-indexing,
(b) if it is algorithmic?

Give worked examples of both.

3 Why do originally unbroken key sequences gradually deteriorate?

4 Describe the most used methods of algorithmic addressing. Compare true randomization with other much-used techniques.

5 Should you try to select an algorithm that does not cause any synonyms to arise?

6   Compare the fitting of the following types of key into (a) division and (b) randomization:

1 Keys in the range $000001 \rightarrow 999999$ into 5841 positions.
2 Keys in the range $539718 \rightarrow 1083919$ into 53424 positions.
3 Keys in the range $AARON \rightarrow ZILLIACUS$ into 54612 positions.
4 Keys in the range $00A12 \rightarrow 99Z37$ into 8916 positions.

7   Explain how to minimize the number of synonyms arising in file loading.

8   Should a full track ever be used as a 'bucket' for direct file purposes?

9   What is the advantage of storing records individually (i.e. not in blocks) in direct files?

10   Compare the effect of one- and two-pass loads in creating synonyms. Give a worked example by inventing a small file and 'loading' it.

11   How can the effect of synonyms be reduced, after their numbers have been minimized?

12   A file holding records singly has been access-frequency loaded to a packing density of 80 per cent. If 90 per cent of accesses are to 10 per cent of records, what improvement will there be over conventional loading? Trace the effect of adding records at random to 90 per cent and 100 per cent packing. You may assume the following:

Record packing density, %	1	2	3	4	5	6	7	8	9	10	80	85	90	95	100
% of records stored as synonyms	0.50	0.99	1.49	1.97	2.46	2.94	3.42	3.90	4.37	4.34	31.17	32.64	34.06	35.45	36.79

13   How is data built up, in order to allow an access-frequency load to be carried out?

14   What sort of files cannot be access-frequency loaded?

15   What sort of file is best suited to access-frequency loading? Justify your comments.

16   What methods of overflow handling are you aware of? Describe the advantages, drawback and necessary precautions involved in using any technique you mention.

17   Why do you think that direct files are not always used in enquiry systems, even though they are able to handle a greater enquiry throughput than any other technique?

7 Indexed-sequential file design

Introduction

Sequential processing with at most very occasional direct reference is best handled by a sequentially organized file. Direct files provide the fastest possible response in an enquiry-only system. The very large number of applications that come somewhere between these two extremes, and require a mixture of direct and sequential reference to data, call for a compromise organization. Indexed-sequential files provide that compromise, so it is not surprising that they are very widely used. We shall first look at ways to optimize their performance.

Optimizing IS files

Manufacturers' software varies, but generally the following facilities are provided:

Direct retrieval of records by the use of indices.

Sequential retrieval, with the opportunity to skip unwanted records.

Addition of records by the provision of overflow areas, and subsequent sequential processing by the use of link fields.

Deletion of records. Sometimes this includes physical removal, sometimes merely tagging (that is, setting a marker in the record) for later deletion; the software treats records as if they had been deleted as soon as they have been tagged.

Statistics that indicate when the file needs to be reorganized.

In order to give these facilities, the make-up of an IS file will usually be as follows:

1. A data storage area, possibly containing some spare space for additions. The lowest-level index elements may also be included in this area.
2. A separate index or indices. An enquiry will reference these indices first, and be pointed to the correct part of the main data file.
3. A separate overflow area.

The provision and position of the indices and overflow areas can dramatically affect file performance.

Indices

In a small file, it might be practical to provide a single index. Any sizeable file is handled by using a hierarchy of indices, each pointing to the next, as this provides more rapid searching and reduced space usage. Readers who wish to examine the reasons for this in detail should consult *Design of Computer Data Files*[1].

The lowest-level index is usually held on the cylinder it refers to, and references the records on a single cylinder, or seek area. There is usually an index entry for each track or bucket of the file. In IBM systems this is called the track index. A full index of every record is seldom if ever justified, as it is not possible to control the precise point on a disk at which the read head will reach the track, so such indices are optional if they are available at all.

The next level of index will point to the cylinder on which the record is stored. There is one entry for each cylinder giving the highest record key on the cylinder, and a scan of the index will allow the next arm movement to be to the required cylinder to retrieve the record. In IBM systems this is called the cylinder index.

When this index exceeds three tracks in size, it is more efficient to create a new index, with one entry per track of the cylinder index, rather than just to increase its size. This is because the new index allows a **direct search** of the main index, rather than a **serial search**. IBM systems allow up to five levels of index to be created; each is justified when the next lower index exceeds three tracks in size, and the software will build such an index automatically unless the user instructs it not to.

In referring to a record directly, the software has to examine two or more indices, and then to search the track on which the record is stored. This process is as follows:

1. Refer to the highest-level index or indices (to locate correct cylinder).
2. Refer to the track index (to determine the correct track).
3. Search the indicated track.

Only the first of these can be optimized. However, as this can cause a long head movement for every reference, the effect can be very marked. Ways of reducing search time are:

1. To hold the highest index in main storage. If this is the cylinder index, all long head movements are avoided and times can be improved by at least 50 per cent. Even if only a higher-level index than the cylinder index is held in main storage, this can improve average access times by 20 per cent or more, as in this case only a single track of the cylinder index has to be searched, not the whole index. Coyle[25] has described the effects of these measures in practice.

   Some manufacturers may allow a part (a half, a third, etc.) of the highest-level index to be held in main storage, which provides a proportionately smaller reduction in average access times.

2. If the highest-level index is too large to be held in main storage, it should be stored on the *fastest available* device. A fixed head disk or a semiconductor 'disk' will provide improvements for two reasons. The first is the speed of the device, the second is the fact that there will not be contention between the cylinder or higher index and the main file area. Disks such as the IBM 3340 or 3350 have optionally a certain amount of fixed head storage, and these indices should be placed on it if it is available.

3. If no high-speed device is available, a *separate* device of the same sort as that used for the main file will reduce head contention, and improve performance. This device should preferably be dedicated to the index during the run in question to avoid head movement.

4. Failing all of these, the higher-level indices will have to be stored in the data file area. If the file is on a single disk pack, the indices should be stored in the *centre* of the file area. If the file occupies several areas on different disks, and nothing is known about the frequency of access to these areas, the cylinder index should be placed in the centre of the smallest file area (and hence, hopefully, the lowest activity area).

When the pattern of accesses to the file is known, conditions change. For a single file area, the cylinder index should be in the centre of the most active area in the file, to minimize head movement. If multiple areas on different packs are in use, the cylinder index should be placed in the centre of the most active part of the least active area. In this way, head movements and contention will be reduced to a minimum.

Correct storing of the high-level indices can dramatically affect retrieval times, as Coyle[25] showed.

Overflow areas

It is sometimes known that a file will have no additions. In this case, no space should be allocated for overflow; generally, however, additions will be expected. The arrangements that can be made for them are as follows:

1. Space can be left in the file area. This can be either within each track or sector, at the end of each cylinder, or a mixture of both. The advantage of this type of overflow is that added records are on the same cylinder as the group of records they belong to, so reference to them does not cause head movements.

2. A separate cylinder or cylinders can be set aside for overflow, and additions to any cylinder can be made into this area. The advantage here is that little space is wasted. The disadvantage is that a head movement is required to retrieve each overflow record.

3. A combination of both the other methods allows a reasonably small space to be set aside within each cylinder, as overflows from the cylinder will be transferred to the independent overflow area.

The method used will depend on the pattern of additions. We shall look at three cases. These are: equal, grouped, and random.

If there are equal numbers of additions to each cylinder, no independent overflow area will be required. Figure 7.1a shows the situation when four

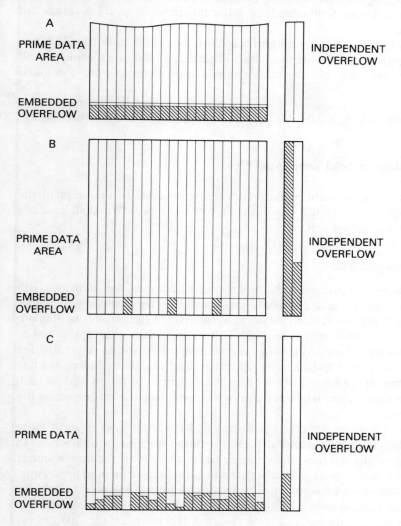

Fig. 7.1 The effect of differing additions patterns to the distribution of overflow records between embedded and independent areas.

records per cylinder are added to a file that has space for five records per cylinder.

When additions are grouped, the main load is in the independent overflow area. Figure 7.1b shows the result when *all* the additions are made to three cylinders.

The most typical case is that of random additions, and the file designer should plan on that basis when nothing is known about the pattern of additions. Figure 7.1c shows a possible pattern in these circumstances. Both the cylinder (embedded) and the independent overflow areas are required.

Additions are made in different ways, but the file designer usually has to go along with the software available. The effect of addition techniques will be examined later, but the reader should use reference 1 for a detailed analysis.

After making decisions on index placement and the strategy to be adopted for additions, the file designer will decide on mode of processing.

Processing indexed-sequential files

Because of their versatility, these files can be processed either sequentially or randomly, presenting the designer with a choice. We shall examine sequential handling first.

Sequential processing

A new or newly reorganized file will not have additions, and all records will be both logically and physically in sequence. The cylinder and higher indices will only be referenced once, at the start of the run. From then on, the only head movements required will be minimum ones at the end of each cylinder. The main loss of time in comparison with a sequential file run will be due to the need to reference the track index before reading every track of the file. This will be counterbalanced by time saved on each occasion that a complete track can be skipped, because no record on the track is required.

In general terms, smaller block sizes and lower hit rates make it more likely that indexed-sequential files will outperform sequential ones. In handling sequential files, the designer needs to know if the manufacturer provides a record storage format that will allow skip-sequential processing, and thus improve sequential run times. Such a format will need to hold the key separate from the main body of a record, so that it can be examined in time for the data to be read in or rejected depending on the value of the key. The details of the two usual record formats for sequential files are given on p. 22. The break-even points for sequential files with separate key

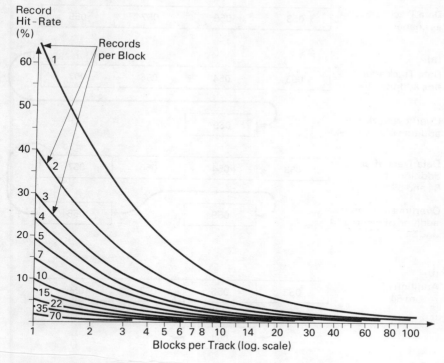

Fig. 7.2 These curves show the approximate break-even points between sequential files with separate key format and indexed-sequential files. Hit-rates *above* a given curve indicate sequential files, while those *below* are more rapidly processed using the indexed-sequential file organization.

format are shown in Fig. 7.2. If the embedded key format is used, IS files have a further advantage.

Additions to the file will lead to the loss of revolutions during sequential processing. During addition of records to IBM's ISAM files, the data track is reorganized so that the record with the highest key of those *logically* on the track is stored in overflow. The whole data track can be scanned sequentially, but the overflow record will cause a lost revolution because the start of the next track in sequence will have been missed by the time it has been read.

Each additional overflow record will cause a further revolution to be lost, as records with lower keys will overflow later, and so will be stored further along the overflow track than higher key records from the same logical track. This is shown in Fig. 7.3a; records with keys 054 and 058 have been added to the track. The first addition requires records 056 and 057 to move up the track, and 059 is pushed into overflow. The second addition goes directly into overflow, and becomes the first in the overflow chain.

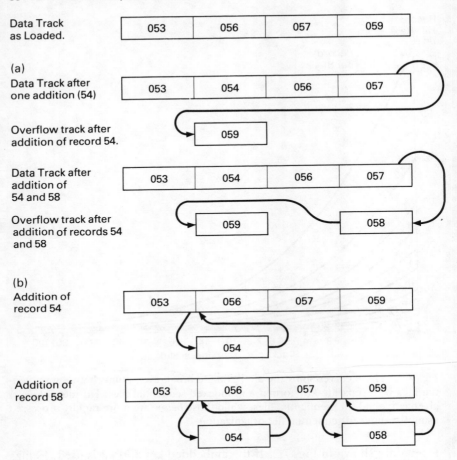

Fig. 7.3 (a) Addition of records to ISAM files. (b) Addition of records to ICL 1900 series indexed-sequential files.

Coyle[25] recommended sorting additions to ISAM files into descending order, and showed that this can reduce both addition and processing times. He also provided 'dummy' records, giving some free space in the home track that was available to hold additions, and thus reduced the number of records in overflow. These two measures improved the number of transactions processed per hour in his case by 50 per cent.

The alternative technique of holding added records in overflow, and linking them directly to the records that precede and follow them in sequence, is shown in Fig. 7.3b. Again, each addition will cause a lost revolution, but in this case the order of additions does not affect timing.

Montgomery and Hubbard[23] have carried out a comparison of IBM and

ICL indexed sequential file organizations, using IBM 2314 disks and the equivalent EDS 30s. This showed that the IBM additions technique provided more rapid sequential retrieval than that used by ICL. As would be expected, the two different file organizations gave virtually identical results in the freshly loaded state; the differences emerged as additions were made.

Direct processing

In order to retrieve a record, each reference will go through the process:

1. Reference to higher index or indices.
2. Reference to track index.
3. Seek record on home track.
4. Follow overflow chain (if necessary).

In the case of records stored in overflow, the fourth step is necessary (although in some circumstances steps 3 and 4 are alternatives—*see* the discussion of ISAM below).

The largest single factor that influences the total retrieval time is step 1. Now that every record retrieval requires a reference to the cylinder index, its location is crucial; this was dealt with on pp. 83–4. In general terms, holding the cylinder index in main storage can reduce the whole process to not much more than half the time required if it is on the same device as the data file. Coyle[25] showed that transfer of the master and, later, cylinder indices to main storage increased throughput for an ISAM file from 12 000 to 22 000 transactions per hour.

Once the position of indices has been optimized, speed of reference depends on the number and position of overflow records. Retrieval of records from independent overflow areas will take significantly more time than from embedded or cylinder overflow areas. The precautions that can be taken in providing overflow areas were discussed on pp. 84–5. The effects are as follows:

First overflow records in ISAM files can be retrieved as rapidly as home records. This is because ISAM track indices hold one prime data record and one overflow record reference per track. When a track has more than one overflow record, this advantage is lost for these additional overflows, as the overflow index record still indicates the key of the last overflow record that is logically part of the track while the address given is now the *first* in the overflow chain. For this reason ISAM software provides the user with a count of the number of references to non-first overflow records during a run.

Linked overflow records will generally require additional time to follow the overflow chain; however, the effect is more dependent on the number of records per block than the number of additions. Montgomery and

Hubbard[23] found that for ICL files, blocks of two records were slightly superior to six-record blocks—random retrieval times of around 65 and 75 ms per record—while 14-record blocks increased individual record retrieval times to about 130 ms.

ISAM files did not show the same sensitivity to number of records per block—two-, six- and 14-record blocks gave retrieval times of around 85, 90 and 95 ms before additions—but they degraded more as records were added. Surprisingly, even in the worst case the retrieval times only degraded by 10–15 per cent when additions made up 40 per cent of the file. Most users have found more rapid degradation than this; these results may be due to the provision of a great deal of overflow space in the data cylinders, which is often not possible.

Process directly or batch and sort?

The ease with which updating of an indexed sequential file can be carried out directly often encourages users to do this. It is true that the need to batch updates and then sort them into order is avoided by this means.

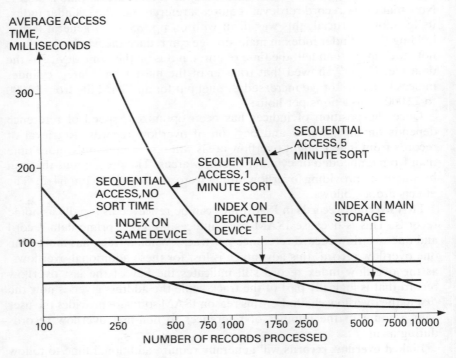

Fig. 7.4 Comparison of the times taken to access records for updating, depending on whether the file is updated directly or input is batched and sorted.

However, direct updating of the file is inherently slower for large numbers of records.

A decision between the two strategies should be based on the size of batch that can be made up—in cases such as payments through the post, this provides a natural batch size. Increasing it by processing only every second or third day imposes an unnecessary delay that should be taken into account in the decision. The storage device used for the file and the time taken to sort updates will also be important.

The situation has been analyzed for an IBM 3330 disk, and described in reference 28. Table 7.1 gives the figures presented there, and Figs. 7.4 and 7.5 show what this means in practice. It is clear that if the cylinder index

Table 7.1 Figures tabulated show the average time in milliseconds required to locate a record.

Number of records	No sort time	One-minute sort	Five-minute sort
	Sequential access times, batched and sorted		
100	175.9	776.4	3176.4
250	75.4	315.4	1275.4
500	41.9	161.9	641.9
750	30.7	110.7	430.7
1000	25.2	85.2	325.1
1750	18.0	52.3	189.4
2500	15.1	39.1	135.1
5000	11.8	23.8	71.8
7500	10.6	18.6	49.3
10000	10.1	16.1	40.1

Direct access times, unbatched records

Cylinder index on the same 3330   101.7
Cylinder index on a dedicated 3330   71.7
Cylinder index in main storage   46.7

Sequential access times have been calculated on the assumption that the disk is accessed, cylinder by cylinder. This sequential scan time is added to the sort time, to give an overall figure that is divided by the number of records to show the time taken to process one record.

can be held in main storage, large batch sizes are required to justify batching and sorting. By comparison, a file that has the cylinder index on the same device as the rest of the file will not justify direct updating even for small batches.

The very marked effect of sort time should be noted. Sorting of a small batch will take a few seconds. Operating overheads may increase this to some minutes, and this should be taken into consideration in the overall decision. If batching and sorting is decided upon, the sort should be

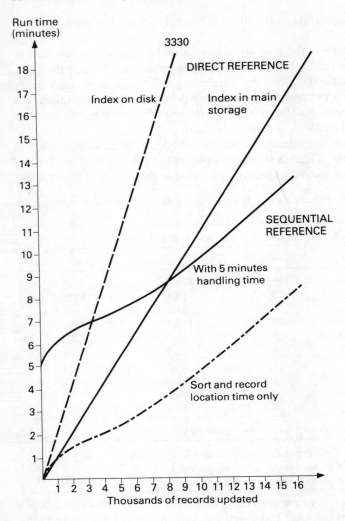

Fig. 7.5 This graph shows the relationship between the number of records to be updated and the run times for direct and batched sequential updating of an indexed-sequential file on an IBM 3330 disk.

handled by job control procedures rather than operator intervention, to minimize lost time.

We have now looked at the operation of well-established indexed-sequential file organization techniques. Weaknesses in these methods have led to a large number of alternatives being offered by software houses, particularly alternatives to IBM's ISAM.

Developments of indexed-sequential files—VSAM and independent software packages

Software provided by manufacturers is aimed at meeting the needs of a very wide spectrum of users. This leads to a general approach to any given problem; the specific requirements of any one application could often be handled more efficiently in some other way, at the expense of other users. This has led to the identification of a number of 'weaknesses' in manufacturers' software that have been remedied by independent software sources.

Because it is very widely used, IBM's ISAM has been the subject of most 'improvement'. The weaknesses in ISAM can be summarized as the use of too much space, and loss of time. The reasons are as follows.

Space

1. Records are unblocked in overflow areas, which means that the file requires more space on the device than if records were blocked.
2. Large user keys may be appropriate for a particular application, but this will increase the size of the indices, allowing less room for data storage and slowing up reference to the indices.
3. Applications requiring both sequential and direct reference will need two separate ISAM modules in main storage. This can use up to 47 k, and may limit the space available to the user program.

Speed

4. Overflow records require longer retrieval times than prime data records. This leads to the need for relatively frequent reorganizations to reduce run times.
5. During sequential processing, a record may not be completely processed until the next record required has passed the read-write heads. A complete disk revolution will elapse before that record is available once more, so considerable time is lost.

Various suppliers have provided software that improves on ISAM in one or more of these areas. The AMIGOS package provided by COMTEN (UK) focused on points (1), (2) and (3). The extra processing time made available by storing data in staggered records is shown in Fig. 7.6. However, the three blocks require *two* revolutions to be processed so that the *average* time may be reduced, but the *minimum* is doubled. PSAM, marketed by Westinghouse Management Systems Division, concentrates on points (1) and (4), by making additions in the prime data area. This is claimed to reduce disk I/O time in comparison with an ISAM file that has records in overflow areas. It also implies that less frequent reorganizations

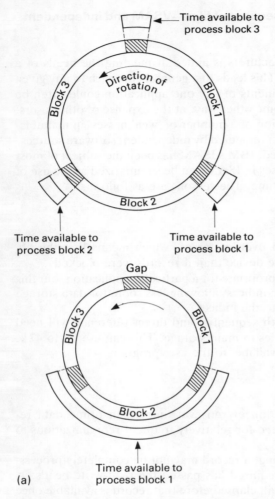

(a)

Fig. 7.6 (a) These diagrams show the time available for processing if records are stored in ascending key sequence. The top diagram illustrates the use of single I/O buffers, while the lower shows double buffers. (b) These diagrams show the increased time that can be made available without losing revolutions if records are stored in staggered sequence; again, the top diagram shows single buffers, the lower diagram double buffers.

are required, and less disk space is used because additions are held in blocked form. It is worth pointing out that ICL's 1900 series indexed sequential software *does* allow the user to specify a packing density of less than 100 per cent for data in the prime data buckets, and so can avoid or drastically reduce the need for separate overflow areas by leaving free space in the data area of the file.

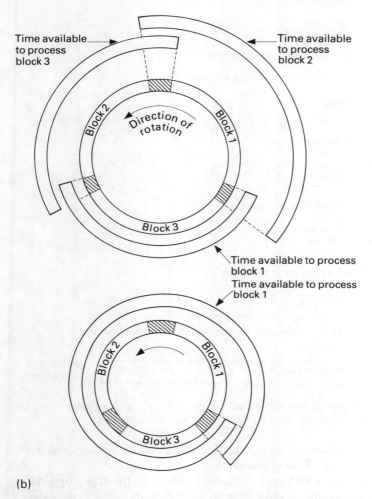

(b)

These instances of 'improved' software can lead users to assume that it is always possible to improve on the performance of a given file. In many cases, this is true, but it does not always apply. The user should first check that manufacturer's software has been fully optimized, using any options that are provided. Coyle[25] examined the performance of an ISAM file in detail, and implemented a series of measures that improved throughput by more than four times. This is shown in Fig. 7.7. He concluded that alternative suppliers did not offer a better solution for his application.

IBM themselves decided to improve on ISAM, and developed VSAM—**Virtual Sequential Access Method**—which takes into account points (1), (2), (4) and (5). In addition, it allows the user to define files without considering the physical make-up of the direct-access storage being used,

| 8000 TRANSA-CTIONS/HOUR | ◄— ORIGINAL THROUGHPUT |

- New records added in descending order

- 'Dummy' records to handle future additions

| 12000 TRANSACTIONS PER HOUR |

- Addition of a master index

| 16000 TRANSACTIONS PER HOUR |

- Master index held in main storage

| 22000 TRANSACTIONS PER HOUR |

- Cylinder index held in main storage

| 28000 TRANSACTIONS PER HOUR |

- Binary search of in-core tables replaces manufacturer's routine (user modification).

| 33000 TRANSACTIONS PER HOUR | ◄— OPTIMISED THROUGHPUT |

Fig. 7.7 These figures demonstrate the improvements Coyle[25] was able to make by using the manufacturer's software options to tune his system.

and to transfer files between different OS/VS operating systems and from OS/VS to DOS/VSE without conversion.

The structure of a VSAM file is shown in Fig. 7.8. In setting up such a file, a key-sequenced file or **data set** is created, with its associated indexes, as a **cluster**. For our purposes the cluster is an indexed file.

Data storage is divided into **control intervals**, which are continuous areas of storage of a size that is not necessarily related to the physical make-up of the device on which the data is stored. This is shown in Fig. 7.9. A control interval is the unit of data that is moved between virtual and backing storage. In a sense, it is equivalent to a track in an ISAM file, in that there is one index entry per control interval.

A group of control intervals makes up a **control area**. The whole of a control area is referenced by the entries in a single index record, and in a sense this is equivalent to a cylinder in ISAM terms.

Indices are arranged as follows: all the higher indices are collectively called the **index set**, and they are divided into index records containing

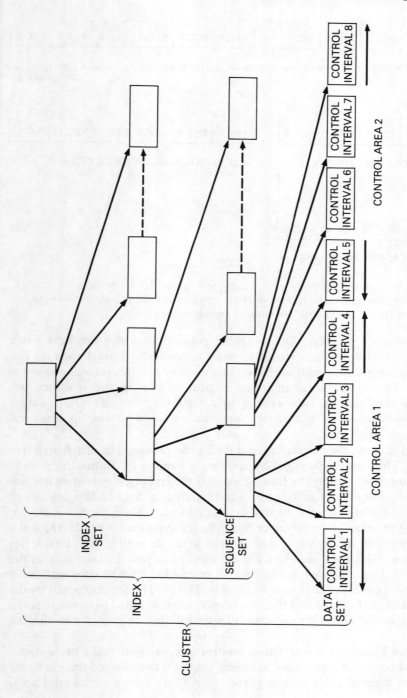

Fig. 7.8 The make-up of a key sequenced VSAM file or cluster.

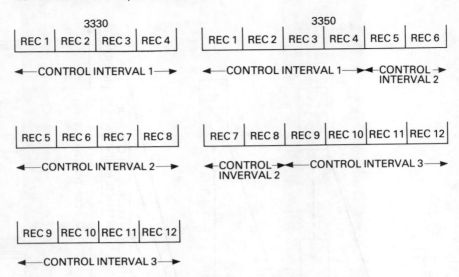

Fig. 7.9 Control intervals are usually best adjusted to the size of a track. However, clusters can be transferred to other devices without redefinition as shown here for IBM's 3330 and 3350, with its greater capacity.

a number of pointers. One of these pointers indicates the next index record at *this* level, and is used to move sequentially through the file. The other pointers indicate the location of a number of index records at a lower level. The lowest level of index records makes up the **sequence set**, and in this case the pointers are to control intervals; the total number of control intervals indexed by one index record makes up a control area.

Additions to the file are catered for by the provision of **distributed free space**. This can be allocated by allowing a number of control intervals to remain entirely empty, by leaving space at the end of every control interval that contains data records, or by a combination of both techniques. As all the space available in a control area is allocated when the file is set up, VSAM provides the equivalent of a cylinder overflow area in ISAM and a proportion of free space in data storage areas, as used in ICL 1900 series software. Records added to a file are blocked in just the same way as the original data, and not unblocked as in ISAM. VSAM does not leave deleted records in the data area, as does ISAM. The area occupied by the record or part of a record that has been deleted is added to the distributed free space available in the control interval that contained the deleted record.

When records are inserted, a **control interval split** takes place under VSAM control if there is not sufficient space for the inserted records in the control interval. This uses any **free** control intervals in the control area, rather than the free space in other control intervals containing data. The consequence of this is that the records may not be physically in sequence after a control interval split, although they will be handled in sequence by the indexes.

If there is not sufficient free space in the control area to handle all additions, a **control area split** takes place under VSAM control. Approximately half the control intervals in the old control area are moved to the new control area, which is made available either as a result of decisions taken when the file was defined, or by extending the file as required. The new control area is likely to be physically remote from the original site of the data. Although VSAM will handle it sequentially, the situation is similar to that of providing an independent overflow area in ISAM, and should be avoided whenever possible.

VSAM provides the possibility of holding **alternate indices**, so the user can reference a file in different sequences using a number of different keys. Alternate indices can be updated when records are added or deleted, by specifying UPGRADE in the alternate index definition. Keys in all VSAM indices are compressed, only the distinguishing parts of the keys being stored, in order to reduce the size of index entries. These facilities make VSAM more similar to database software than most of the file organization techniques that have been examined so far—in fact, many of the 'database' systems available for mini- and microcomputers provide only this multiple index facility.

VSAM can be optimized by careful design, applying the same principles that have been described earlier. The designer should look at the following factors:

1. The relation of data areas and index position to the physical characteristics of the device. The portability of a VSAM file from one device to another, and from operation under one OS/VS system to another, or from OS/VS to DOS/VSE is helpful in providing rapid conversion. However, for optimum performance the size of control intervals and control areas should be so arranged that a sequence set record will be stored on the same cylinder as the control area it indexes. This means that movement from, say, a 3330 to a 3350 will require the definition of new control area sizes unless the number of control areas on a cylinder has been designed to take account of this future change of disk.

   Control areas stored *two* per cylinder on a 3330 will move without loss of efficiency to a 3350, *three* per cylinder; *single* control areas on a 3330 cylinder would lead to inefficiency on a 3350, because one and a half control areas on a cylinder would separate some index records and part of their control areas (*see* Fig. 7.9).
2. The size of the buffers provided for VSAM directly determines the number of higher index records held in virtual storage (as against

backing storage). Hence buffers should be both as large as possible, and related in size to index record size.

3. Distribution of free space. The ability to define empty control intervals where they are required means that careful planning with a knowledge of the likely distribution of additions will reduce the need for control area splits, and possibly of control intervals splits. This will improve performance. Further details of VSAM are available in IBM publications.

Conclusion

Indexed-sequential files are often taken for granted, because the manufacturers provide comprehensive software. Optimization of this software can bring very substantial benefits. In some cases, software from independent suppliers will be more suitable, because its design aims match the needs of a given application. Professional file designers should be in a position to optimize manufacturers' software, and decide when to try alternatives in order to attain some objective that the supplied software is not capable of providing.

VSAM is a departure towards database software. In some of the following chapters, we shall examine the development of this software, its advantages and penalties.

Revision questions

1 Explain the likely uses of sequential, indexed sequential and direct files in data processing, making clear when you would use each of them, and when there might be some difficulty in deciding between them.

2 What facilities are generally provided by manufacturers' indexed sequential software?

3 Describe the make up of an IS file, explaining what parts of it have to be present and what parts are optional.

4 Design a set of indices for an IS file, showing how they are arranged, and giving sufficient detail to demonstrate the comparisons needed to retrieve directly a number of records that you have set in the file. Explain the reasons for a hierarchy of indices, giving examples to substantiate the reasons you give.

5 How does index placement affect the performance of IS files? Explain the options open to the file designer, and outline the reasons there might be for making any given choice.

6   Explain the options available for providing for overflow in an IS file, and give examples of files that might need any *one* or *multiple* options.

7   If manufacturer's software does not allow the provision of *distributed free space*, how could you arrange to provide it?

8   Compare the use of sequential and IS files for sequential processing. What conditions favour the use of IS files? Explain the reasons for your answer.

9   Explain the effect of additions to an IS file on sequential processing. Compare addition and deletion handling. Why the difference (if any)?

10   What are the steps needed to retrieve a record directly? How do overflow records differ from those in the prime data area?

11   When should an IS file be processed directly, and when should input be batched and sorted. How would you determine a break-even point?

12   Why was VSAM introduced? What does it offer that ISAM does not?

13   When should you consider an alternative to the manufacturers' IS software? Mention some packages you know of, and what they offer.

14   Describe the structure of a VSAM file.

15   Describe the steps taken by Coyle in optimizing an ISAM file, and explain the improvement he obtained. How does it compare with the claims made by independent suppliers? What comment have you on the comparison?

8 Inverted files and information retrieval

Most data processing applications use a single record key, or at most a limited number of keys. The type of application in which a selection is made from a set of records, based on some combination of requirements, is an exception to this. There are no longer any particular 'keys' as such; instead, the record has to be searched using some combination of keys (often called **attributes**) provided by the user.

Applications

Typical selection applications are personnel or library handling. In the first case, a group of FEMALE employees who can SPEAK GERMAN and are UNDER THIRTY might be required. Employee records would be scanned, using the boolean conditions (female) AND (speaks German) AND (under thirty). Records satisfying all three requirements would be selected.

The keys above are fairly definite, although 'can speak German' may prove to be a variable ability. In library applications, keys are far more subjective. The easy way to define keys is to use the significant words in the title. However, titles may be intended to be striking rather than informative. Even author abstracts can be misleading, as there is a natural tendency for the author to concentrate on positive achievements rather than negative findings, and so not to be objective.

The safe way to select appropriate keys is to have each article, book, etc, examined by an information specialist in the field, in order to allocate the keys. Despite this, information retrieval is likely to lead to some irrelevant articles being selected and some relevant ones being missed, however much care is taken in choice of keywords.

Selection of records will be on the basis of boolean conditions such as AND, OR, BUT NOT IF. There should also be provisions to broaden an inquiry if no records match the original conditions, or to narrow it if too many records are selected.

Order of keys is also important—MANAGEMENT INFORMATION SYSTEMS are not usually INFORMATION MANAGEMENT SYSTEMS. Other desirable facilities are that synonyms should be acceptable.

For example:

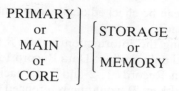

$$\left.\begin{array}{c} \text{PRIMARY} \\ \text{or} \\ \text{MAIN} \\ \text{or} \\ \text{CORE} \end{array}\right\} \left\{\begin{array}{c} \text{STORAGE} \\ \text{or} \\ \text{MEMORY} \end{array}\right.$$

gives six possible synonyms for main storage (PRIMARY STORAGE, PRIMARY MEMORY, MAIN STORAGE, MAIN MEMORY, CORE STORAGE, CORE MEMORY). Root words such as INTEGRA*** should yield a hit with integral, integrate, integrated, etc.

Possible file organizations

Computer systems that provide these functions require specialist files and record formats. All possible keys must be in a predetermined position or sequence, in order to allow searching to be carried out. The format depends on the type of file used.

The simplest arrangement of records is to store them in order, with the record first, followed by all its keys, in the format shown in Fig. 8.1a. This

(a)

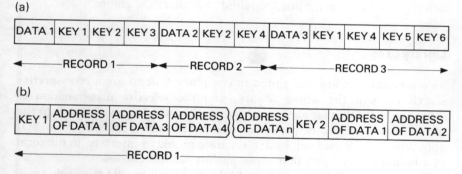

(b)

Fig. 8.1 (a) Serial file. Note that keys may be used in more than one record. (b) Inverted file. Note that data will be referred to by the records for each of its keys but the data will only be stored in complete form once.

file organization has the advantage that addition of new records is straightforward; they are added at the tail of the file. It is also convenient for boolean testing, as the records are examined one by one to see if their keys meet the conditions laid down.

The disadvantage of this method is that every record in the file has to be examined, to deal with a single inquiry. When files are small this is not a drawback, but when there are 20 000 to 30 000 records the time taken is so long that it is better to use a different file organization.

In order to avoid scanning every record, the keys and data can be organized as shown in Fig. 8.1b. Using this 'inverted' arrangement, the keys given in an inquiry can be checked one by one, and only the relevant keys have to be referenced.

For example, using the information in Fig. 8.1a, the inquiry (Key 1) AND (Key 2) would only produce Data Record 1, while (Key 1) OR (Key 2) would yield Data Records 1, 2 and 3. In each case only two records (those for Key 1 and Key 2) would be referenced. This compares with the scan of the entire file that would be needed if a serial file organization were being used.

If the file is large, the inverted file organization allows a far greater volume of inquiries to be handled than is possible using a serial file.

Inverted files pose an update problem, in that records throughout the file are changed when a new data record is added, if any of the keys of the new record have been used previously for any other record. As the file grows larger some duplication of keys becomes virtually certain, and the addition of a new record will involve updating many different data records. Larger work areas are needed for boolean operations than in the serial file case, which limits the complexity of the logical expressions that are possible.

For many applications—personnel, computer dating, etc—choice of file organization is a matter of file size. The typical library application is rather different, in that the facilities required also affect the choice.

Library uses

Two services that are well suited to computer systems are a **retrospective search** through the whole library, and the **selective dissemination of information** (SDI) that aims to let users know which new additions to the library collection are of particular interest to them personally. For SDI applications each user will have a separate profile of interests, in the form of a boolean expression that is run against new accessions.

The two are different in that an SDI service will handle relatively small files, while a retrospective search is usually only carried out on fairly large files. A number of commercial systems use the technique shown in Fig. 8.2 to batch input, so that updating of the main file, which is held in inverted form, is relatively infrequent.

These services can be useful for personnel type applications, but their main use is in libraries, where a further problem will be the relevance of the retrieved information to the person who requested it.

Standard accession lists containing every new item are often discarded by users because pages of irrelevant material have to be read in order to become aware of a handful of additions to the library that are of interest. However, most users would accept one useful article in three or four, and thus a relatively low **relevance**, defined as (number of relevant documents) ÷ (number of documents retrieved). The aim of a computer-

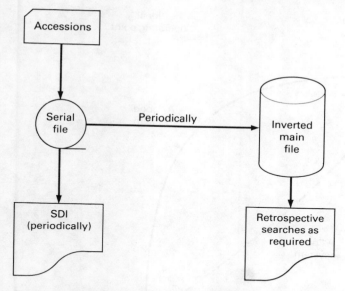

Fig. 8.2 A system that uses both serial and inverted files. The main file need not be updated with the same frequency that SDI reports are provided.

based information retrieval system should be to achieve this level of relevance, as against the 1 in 20 to 1 per 100 of the typical accession list.

Missing relevant articles, because they are not retrieved by the system, constitute a more serious problem. This is measured by **recall**, defined as (number of relevant articles retrieved) ÷ (number of relevant articles present in the full collection). As the user gets no indication of articles the system has failed to locate, it is important that most of the relevant articles should be retrieved, even if this means that the relevance of the listing offered to the user is lowered.

A system will give different results for different inquiries, but the curves in Fig. 8.3, which show the relationship between relevance and recall in two hypothetical systems, are typical of good and bad systems in operation.

Measurements of these values are not in any sense fixed; the care and accuracy with which a user's profile of interests has been framed will affect the response the system gives. The ability of the information scientists who decided what keywords were appropriate for a given article will determine whether it is retrieved under the correct conditions. Despite this, systems usually show a relationship between relevance and recall similar to those in Fig. 8.3, reflecting their overall level of discrimination.

Ideally, the system would operate at 100 per cent recall and 100 per cent relevance. No existing system can offer this, and in order to ensure a high degree of recall—because the user cannot know what information has not

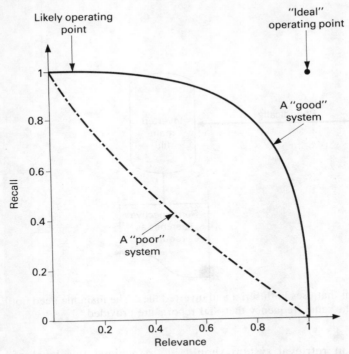

Likely operating point

"Ideal" operating point

A "good" system

A "poor" system

Recall

Relevance

Fig. 8.3 A system is usually run with high recall and relatively low relevance to avoid loss of information.

been offered to him—it is usual to operate with a relatively low relevance, of the order of 15 per cent to 30 per cent.

The relevance of a system can be reviewed constantly by asking users to assess it. Recall can only be checked by arranging for helpful and long-suffering users to scan the whole collection of additions at intervals, to discover how many relevant articles have not been selected by the system.

Conclusion

Inverted files are useful in any case where multiple keywords in combination are required to select a record. They merit consideration by the file designer for many data processing applications.

Revision questions

1 When is a single key not useful in retrieving a record?

2 Describe the considerations involved in selecting records using multiple keys.

3 Explain the make-up, strengths and weaknesses of a sequential information retrieval file.

4 What is an inverted file? Compare its strengths and weaknesses with those of a sequential information retrieval file.

5 What is a retrospective search? When is it required?

6 Define SDI. In what way would two users' references differ?

7 Explain *relevance* and *recall*. How would you check them in a given system?

8 Describe a system providing both SDI and retrospective search, emphasizing the types of secondary storage required for the files you need.

9 Discuss the efficiency of the system you have described in various conditions of relevance and recall. What are the merits of choosing a given operating point, and how would you do it?

10 Are inverted files only useful in library applications? If you think not, explain any other applications you feel they might be appropriate for, and why.

9 Special-purpose files

Special-purpose files can be divided into two groups. The first includes those files designed by users to meet their own specific needs, while the second is made up of specialist software provided by manufacturers or software houses to handle applications such as production planning.

User-designed files

An example of user-designed files is the case where there is a requirement for very rapid running of a sequential file. Direct-access devices have higher transfer rates than magnetic tapes, and in addition it is possible to almost eliminate waiting time before a record is available by using these devices correctly.

Inter-block gap times on tapes, however, cannot be avoided (although the time lost can, of course, be overlapped with other processing). For this reason, rapid-transfer sequential files are usually held on direct-access devices.

High transfer speeds can be achieved if processing is minimal—copy disk or clear disk, for example—as the processing is carried out during the time the read–write heads traverse the very small inter-record gap (equivalent to the transfer time for 56–180 characters from disk). In most cases, processing times will be too long to allow this overlap; by the time the first record has been processed, the start of the second record will already have passed the read–write heads and it is no longer possible to read it in directly.

Usually, this will lead to a number of lost revolutions; this can be avoided by arranging the file as shown in Fig. 9.1.

In this case, the dummy records are made just long enough to allow processing and writing of the first record before the second becomes available, processing and writing of the second before the third becomes available, and so on.

Double buffering allows more time for processing and writing records, and cuts down the amount of space needed for dummy records. This is also shown in Fig. 9.1. These dummies still waste a good deal of direct access storage, however, which has led to a further development of the technique.

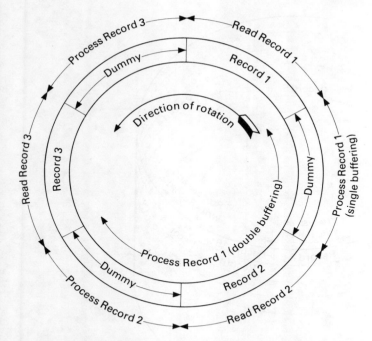

Fig. 9.1 The arrangement of data records and dummy records on a track to ensure that no time is wasted due to rotational delay. If double buffers are used, Record 1 is available for processing and writing back until Record 3 is read.

Spiral files are arranged as shown in Fig. 9.2. The first record is stored at the start of the first track, the second is placed far enough along the second track to ensure that it is not read until the processing and writing back of Record 1 is complete. Records are arranged on descending tracks in sequence until a record is reached that can be 'fitted into' Track 1 closely following Record 1. In Fig. 9.2, this is Record 8, and the spiral is repeated from this point.

The packing of data records that can be achieved is usually about 90 per cent but only in very fortunate cases can all the space on direct-access storage be utilized.

Files designed on these or similar principles can produce very short run times, as rotational delays are virtually eliminated. However, such files suffer from two serious drawbacks.

The first is that they are device-dependent, and their performance can be ruined by transfer to another device. The second is that the processing involved cannot be varied; once the file is 'tuned' to give optimum performance, no additional jobs can be carried out without redesigning the file to adjust record positions. This means that such files are only suitable in

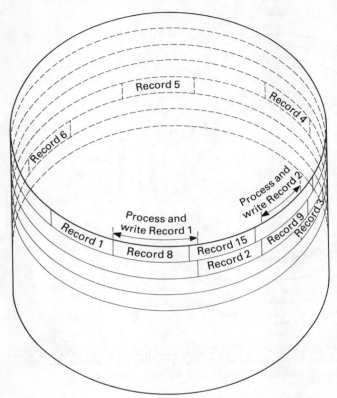

Fig. 9.2 Records are arranged in a spiral pattern, the first on Track 1, the second on Track 2, and so on, until rotation of the disk allows a further record, in this case Record 8, to be placed on Track 1 following Record 1 as closely as possible.

a few cases, and are always 'brittle' and invariable. Nowadays, such files are more likely to be created by microcomputer users rather than mainframe users.

Proprietary software

The second class of specialist files is very different. In recent years, the use of computers in production control, production scheduling, calculation of materials processing requirements and the like, has become an important part of data processing. Applications of this type often require complex chained or linked files. A reference to a particular machined part, for example, can be used to provide a list of the processes it passes through in the course of manufacture, or a breakdown of the assemblies it is used in, and in what quantities, in the manufacture of a finished product.

Variation of these options will allow an application to be effectively tuned, but it is important to start from a known base and the minimum option set is the most convenient.

The user systems analyst responsible for such an application will be more involved in choice of alternatives than in true file design. Each manufacturer offers a distinctive set of products, and familiarity with a given package will allow the user to choose a minimum set of options that meets his requirements.

A serious trap lies in wait for the systems analyst here. It is best illustrated by an example.

CLASS, Capacity Loading and Scheduling System, is a program that was developed by IBM Germany but which has since been superseded by newer IBM software. It was designed to schedule work more efficiently, and to reduce the amount of work-in-progress (WIP) on the shop-floor.

Management see WIP as capital and added value lying idle in the factory. Any method of reducing the quantity of cash locked up in WIP and thus not available to the company is attractive to management. The use of the CLASS program thus automatically offered any company the possibility of cash benefits. However, the individual machine-minder sees WIP as his guarantee of there being a job for him next week. Unless he is convinced a system that cuts WIP will benefit him, shop-floor morale is endangered by any such system and repercussions must be expected.

One company that installed CLASS found that initial reductions in WIP were followed by a general reduction in productivity, which resulted in WIP returning to levels similar to those that applied before CLASS was installed. Several cycles of this type resulted in the removal of the CLASS program from the installation. However, the failure was not a technical one. The systems analysts responsible for the program had not communicated with shop-floor workers to ensure that they knew what to expect—a reduced level of WIP—and to explain that this was not a threat to their jobs, but part of an operation intended to make them more secure. The price of this omission was failure.

The file designer is not only responsible for the technical side of his work. In addition, he must allow for its impact on other members of the organization, and ensure that they expect, and accept, the changes his work will cause.

Revision questions

1 Why would a user wish to write a file organization for a specific application?

2 Explain the reasons why a high transfer-rate sequential file is usually held on disk. What effect does single or double buffering of input/output records have on this application?

3 Describe the design of a spiral file. What are the advantages of such a file? What are its disadvantages?

4 What type of computer might now use a spiral file design?

5 What applications might be handled by specialist file organization techniques provided by manufacturers?

6 What does the user do with manufacturer's specialist file software? What is involved in optimizing such a software system?

7 Describe the precautions a file designer should take in ensuring that a specialist file system is successfully implemented.

8 Compare the use of specialist file software with the more standard file organization techniques. How much work must the user put into each application? What about the file designer's responsibility?

10 File design for on-line systems†

Introduction

In this chapter we shall examine some of the practical factors which need to be considered when designing the file system for an on-line environment, in addition to those covered under the chapters on the specific file organizations.

There are two fundamental design parameters for any on-line system: availability and response time. For example, we may say that a given system has to provide a mean response time of 2 s or less with an availability of 90 per cent, in order to be acceptable to its users. These design parameters need to be translated into a design involving the files, programs, terminal equipment, etc. that the system will use. Though we shall mainly be concerned with the file system, the techniques that will be covered are relevant to the other aspects of on-line system design.

Availability

The availability of any component or system is defined by the following ratio (known as α):

$$\alpha = \frac{\text{mean time to fail (MTF)}}{\text{mean time to fail (MTF)} + \text{mean time to repair (MTR)}}$$

Thus if the mean time to fail of a disk unit were 1000 h of use, and the mean time to repair were 5 h, the availability of the unit would be $\alpha = 1000/1005 = 0.995$ or 99.5 per cent. Calculation of the MTF and MTR may be carried out in practice by observation and measurement, though if new equipment is being considered it is necessary to obtain figures from the manufacturer. This is often difficult, since manufacturers are reluctant to reveal these figures. An important aspect to consider in calculating the MTR is any waiting time before an engineer actually arrives on site to repair the equipment. Even if it only takes 10 min to change a defective circuit board, if the engineer takes 2 h to arrive then the MTR is 2 h 10 min.

† Contributed by Norman Revell, Senior Tutor, The Centre for Business Systems Analysis, The City University, London

(This illustrates one of the benefits of a resident engineer if the installation is large enough to justify one.)

In considering the application of reliability factors to the design of an on-line system, the principle that 'a chain is only as strong as its weakest link' applies. An on-line system may be viewed as a chain of subsystems, each of which must be working for the total system to function correctly, and the elements in a typical system are shown in Fig. 10.1.

Fig. 10.1 Typical reliability chain for an on-line system.

Suppose that we have a system of just two elements whose availabilities α_1 and α_2 are known (see Fig. 10.2). From probability theory, the

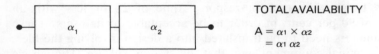

Fig. 10.2 A series connection of units.

availability of the system A is $\alpha_1 \times \alpha_2$. Thus if each element had an availability of 90 per cent, the system availability would be 81 per cent.

In order to make the system more reliable it is necessary to duplex the weaker parts of it. If a duplicate element is provided, the probability of *either* element *not* being available is $(1 - \alpha)$ and the probability of *neither* being available is $(1 - \alpha)^2$; thus the duplexed availability is $1 - (1 - \alpha)^2 = \alpha(2 - \alpha)$. For example, if we duplex a system element whose availability is 90 per cent, the duplexed availability becomes $0.9(2 - 0.9) = 0.99$ or 99 per cent. This is shown in Fig. 10.3, where the

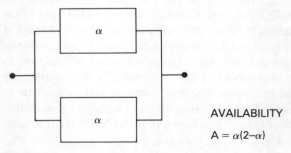

Fig. 10.3 A parallel (duplexed) connection of units.

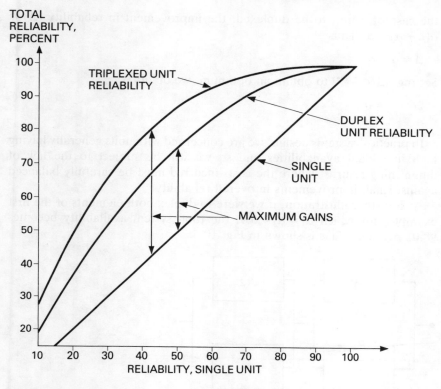

Fig. 10.4 Reliability graphs for single, duplexed and triplexed units.

normal convention of showing duplicated elements in parallel is illustrated. As an aid to the designer, Fig. 10.4 shows a graph of availabilities of units which are duplexed and triplexed. It is seldom necessary to go beyond this latter stage—in fact, very few systems go this far. The US Space Launch Mission Control System and airline reservation systems have components triplexed, but duplexing is generally sufficient for most DP use unless there is some extremely unreliable element in a system. One thing apparent from Fig. 10.4 is the 'law of diminishing returns'—at high levels of unit reliability the improvement in overall reliability becomes very marginal. In fact, the graph reveals that there is an optimum reliability figure for either duplexing or triplexing which gives the greatest gain in overall reliability. For a unit to be duplexed, this figure is 50 per cent availability—at availabilities higher or lower than this the improvement in total reliability is less. For a unit to be triplexed, the figure is 42.3 per cent, while for a unit already duplexed which is to be triplexed it is 33 per cent. Any of these figures may be derived analytically from the reliability formulae; for example, taking the case of a unit to be duplexed, the improvement in reliability (Δ) is $\alpha(2 - \alpha) - \alpha$. Thus

$$\Delta = \alpha - \alpha^2$$

Setting $d\Delta/d\alpha = 0$ to obtain an optimum, we obtain

$$2\alpha - 1 = 0$$
$$\alpha \quad = 0.5$$

In practical systems design, we are concerned with units generally having high individual availabilities and so we will be subject to the law of diminishing returns, where the costs incurred must be carefully balanced against small improvements in overall reliability.

As a further illustration, if we were to duplex both elements of the first example, for which $\alpha_1 = \alpha_2 = 0.9$, the total system availability becomes 98.01 per cent. This is shown in Fig. 10.5.

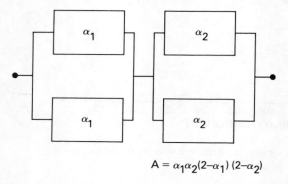

$$A = \alpha_1 \alpha_2 (2-\alpha_1)(2-\alpha_2)$$

Fig. 10.5 A system of two elements with duplexing.

Using these two basic building blocks of series and parallel connection, the reliability network for complex configurations can be drawn up and total availabilities calculated.

When designing the files subsystem for an on-line system, the same principle applies. For example, suppose we had two banks, each of four disk drives, and each bank was connected to the CPU via a fully switchable channel and control unit. Further, let us suppose that the files to be referenced occupy a whole bank of drives and that the application requires all of these files to be available. Using the availabilities shown in Fig. 10.6, a total disk subsystem availability is derived, which is given in the figure itself.

In this example, the fourth power of α_D makes the disk bank the 'weak link' of the system. In practice, therefore, it is important to design the files so that a 'graceful degradation' is possible, and not to have the rather

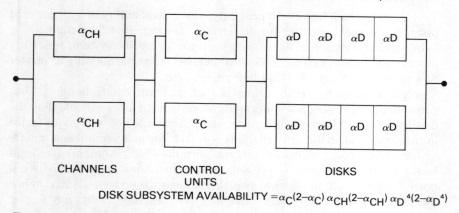

$$\text{DISK SUBSYSTEM AVAILABILITY} = \alpha_C(2-\alpha_C)\,\alpha_{CH}(2-\alpha_{CH})\,\alpha_D{}^4(2-\alpha_D{}^4)$$

Fig. 10.6 A typical disk file subsystem.

stringent requirement that all of the disk drives should need to be available for the system to function. If the master files were spread over the disks in such a way that only part of the system were lost, then it would be possible to continue processing after a single disk failure. Also, if all the drives were made switchable between both control units, the system would be much more resilient.

A basic design question which needs to be answered is: 'Which element is it best to duplex?' Using the formula previously derived, the relative improvement in reliability obtained by duplexing an element is given by $(2 - \alpha)$. Thus, an element whose availability is 90 per cent would improve overall system availability by 10 per cent if it were duplexed. As would be expected, the biggest gain is to be derived by duplexing the 'weakest link', but this is not the complete picture; an important item to consider is cost.

When considering reliability improvements, it is possible to work out the 'best buy' option by dividing the cost of each element by the percentage improvement in system availability obtained through duplexing. For example, a disk controller costing £10 000 and having availability of 99 per cent would provide a 1 per cent improvement in system availability at a cost of £10 000; a disk drive having a reliability of 90 per cent at a cost of £3000 would provide an improvement of 10 per cent at a cost of £300 per cent.

A further factor which should be considered as part of the costing is the degree of redundancy. If the element duplexed is being used for some other application, an allowance should be made for this when costing the effect of duplexing as outlined above. This same principle can, of course, be applied to triplexing or even quadruplexing vital elements in a configuration, though the benefits are likely to be very marginal for most commercial systems. For a unit which is triplexed, the availability is

$1 - (1 - \alpha)^3$, which for $\alpha = 90$ per cent gives an availability of 99.9 per cent (as opposed to 99 per cent for duplexing). *See* Fig. 10.4 for details.

In making a choice of file organization for an on-line system, reliability theory calculations can be applied to such factors as partitioning of master files, using a separate disk holding indices, etc.

A practical point worth noting is that with current technology, disk controllers and channels will normally be very much more reliable than the drive units which have moving parts, and thus should not be a major factor in the design calculation of reliability—in fact, for many 'mini' and 'micro' systems these components are integral with the CPU. Another significant factor to be considered is software reliability—something which is not normally duplexed, though the availability factor could be measured in just the same way that hardware reliability is measured. Gilb[40] has in fact suggested the handling of software reliability in this way.

To summarize, we have seen how reliability calculations can influence the file hardware configuration, and the organization of the files, in an on-line system. There is nothing to prevent the same techniques being used for a batch system where a requirement for high availability exists—it is just that much higher MTRs can normally be tolerated in batch systems. Reference 38 provides a more detailed discussion of the above point whilst reference 41 in particular analyzes cost factors.

Response time

The previous section examined the way in which reliability calculations can influence the design of the file for an on-line system. In this section, we look at the second design parameter for an on-line system—that of response—and examine the effect it has on choice of file organization.

First, we shall develop a simple queuing model which can be used to calculate the response time for a system that is processing transactions which arrive at random.

Suppose we have an on-line system where n transactions per second arrive randomly distributed, and each transaction requires t references to a disk file whose mean access time (seek plus search plus data transfer) is d ms. **Response time** is defined as the total of both the time spent queuing and being served, i.e. the total time a transaction spends in that part of the system. The general single-server queuing theory formula for the mean response time, given random arrival time and service time distributions, is

$$T = s/(1 - p)$$

where T is the response time, s is the mean service time and p is the facility utilization.

Service time is the time taken to complete the transaction ignoring the effect of all other transactions and is a measure of the actual resource requirements. For example, in the case of a disk drive, this will be the average access time (seek, search plus data transfer). In the above formula, it is assumed to be an average, which is more typical of data processing systems than other formulae which assume constant service times for example.

Facility utilization is defined as the ratio of

$$\frac{\text{time in use}}{\text{time available for use}}$$

It is often known as the **load factor**.

In this example, the facility utilization is given by $ntd/1000$ and so the response time for each disk reference becomes

$$T = \frac{d}{1 - (ntd/1000)} \text{ ms}$$

Figure 10.7 shows a series of curves of response times for different values

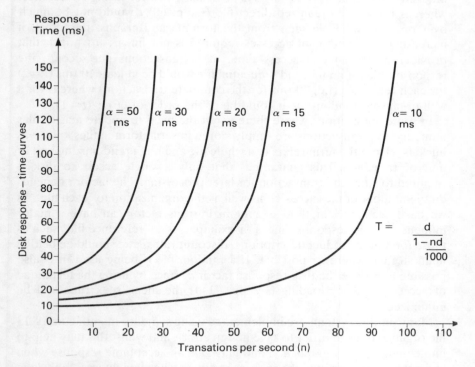

Fig. 10.7 Disk response-time curves. Note that $t = 1$ for these curves.

of disk access times in the case where $t = 1$. It is interesting to note how modest the loading needs to be, to bring about a response time of double the service time (50 per cent in fact), whereas intuitively it would seem reasonable to allow greater load factors than this. At very high load factors, response times would grow extremely long (as anyone queuing at a supermarket at a busy period knows). There is a further penalty, in that transactions queuing in the system need buffers to store them, otherwise terminal keyboard lockouts will occur (i.e. the system is unable to accept any new input data from terminals and the keyboard locks pending the transmission of data that is already waiting in the terminal buffer).

The effect of file organization and structure

In practice, when an on-line system is being designed, the response time has been specified, and the designer has to choose an appropriate file organization and disk hardware to meet this time for specified transaction volumes. The choice of file organization will affect the number of references t per transaction. For example, if the file being referenced were indexed-sequential, t would always be at least two for a single reference, whereas for a well-organized direct file (*see* p. 60) t would not be much over one. As we have seen from the formula and graphs, the effect of increasing the number of accesses required is not linear: for a disk that provides a 50 ms mean access time, at 5 transactions per second, the response time for an indexed sequential file would be at least 100 ms ($t = 2$) for each reference (i.e. 200 ms for the complete transaction) whereas for a well-organized random file it could be of the order of 66 ms ($t = 1$).

In some applications where there is not the need to update master files immediately, transactions are simply stored in serial form in files known as **buckets**. (Here the term refers to a whole file and not a randomizing unit or unit of transfer.) This guarantees that only a single access to disk is required to store the transaction for later processing. The factor t depends on the number of files accessed as well as the organization for each file. As we have seen, any method of minimizing this factor can have a major influence on the response time. For example, small reference files such as those found for product descriptions, discount rates, etc. should be held in main storage wherever possible. If a random file is being used, it is also possible to reduce the disk response factor d, since by using the technique of access-frequency loading (*see* pp. 71–4) the mean seek time will be minimized.

Many on-line systems are implemented using standard manufacturers' IS file organizations in order to save design effort, and whilst this may help to implement the system quickly, and may give an acceptable response when the system first goes live, the response time may become unacceptably long as the volume of transactions increases. A conversion to direct organization will then be necessary in order to avoid the purchase of additional and/or faster disks. The pros and cons of the two different purchase alternatives are discussed below.

The choice of file hardware

The other factor over which the designer often has control is the choice of disk hardware. Suppose the file organizations have been optimized as described in the previous section, how may the designer then proceed to select the disk units required to meet a target response figure? Given a knowledge of the other variables, it is possible to calculate the mean access time of disk required for a given application using the formula

$$d = \frac{T}{1 + (nTt/1000)} \text{ ms}$$

which is derived from the previous formula for T.

Table 10.1 shows the disk file requirements at three different response levels necessary to maintain a given transaction volume. For example, if we wish to maintain a 500 ms response time for 50 transactions per second, then we will require a disk drive with a mean access time of 19 ms or better.

Table 10.1 Mean access time d tabulated for given volumes and response requirements.

Transactions/s	$T = 100\,ms$	$T = 200\,ms$	$T = 500\,ms$
10	50	$66\frac{2}{3}$	83.3
20	33.3	40	45.5
30	25	28.6	31.25
45	20	22.2	23.8
50	16.6	18.2	19.2
66	14.33	15.4	16.1
70	12.5	13.3	13.9
80	11.1	11.8	12.2
90	10	10.5	10.9
100	9.09	9.5	9.8

Another design decision has to be reached when a system is becoming heavily loaded and a choice has to be made between replacing the disk drive(s) by a faster one or spreading the files over extra drives (thus reducing the load factor n). Let us take as a simple example a case where a single disk drive holds an on-line file, and there is a choice of either splitting the file across two drives or acquiring a single drive twice as fast (half the mean disk response time d). The first option gives a response

$$T = \frac{d}{1 - (ntd/2000)}$$

where for the second option of a faster disk drive we have

$$T = \frac{d/2}{1 - (ntd/2000)}$$

Thus the response time of the second option is only half that of the first and so on the basis of response alone it is better to opt for a faster drive. In practice, there will be other considerations such as the higher availability of the first option and relative costs and capacities, but this calculation does provide an example of how the theory may be applied to the performance aspect of the decision.

The simple single-server, queuing model used in this chapter has made certain assumptions about distributions of arrival times and service times; in practice, these will amount to approximations since there may be 'bunching' of transactions and the accesses to disk may not be entirely at random. Nevertheless, the theory provides a good first approximation, and if a more accurate calculation is required then it is necessary to use more advanced theory or build a simulation model—an effort usually only justified where load factors, etc, are known with great precision, as otherwise greater errors are likely to accrue due to bad estimates!

As with the reliability calculations covered earlier, queuing theory has wider applications than just the file design factors covered here. An example is the design of a teleprocessing system where equipment response must be calculated and included in the total response time figure. The application to batch file processing systems is more limited, since in a batch system there is an orderly flow of transactions through the system, though if a batch program were multi-tasking transactions for the same file, or multiprogramming caused a high degree of contention for a given disk drive, it is possible that queues may develop (in just the same way that queues are built and managed by some operating systems). It is doubtful that these events are as accurately represented by a random arrival pattern as are the queues caused by the terminal operators of an on-line system all working independently (*see* reference 39) if only because terminal systems may have hundreds of separate users at any given time.

Conclusion

Both reliability theory and queuing theory are valuable techniques to the designer since they are able to provide a quantitative basis for decisions otherwise often made on a rule-of-thumb basis; in common with other techniques discussed in this book, neither require a great deal of time to perform. For greater precision, simulation—possibly with the use of hardware monitoring—may be of value, though the design effort to use this technique is considerably greater.

Finally, it is important to remember that the two are independent—investment to bring about a better response time does not necessarily improve system availability or vice versa.

Revision questions

1 The MTF for floppy disk drives is normally 10 000 h or more. Discuss the implications of this on the practical operation of a business microcomputer with two disk drives.

2 Two disk drives each having availabilities of 90 per cent have MTFs of 9 h and 90 h respectively with MTRs of 1 h and 10 h. Discuss their use in an environment working (a) 1 h a day, (b) 16 h a day.

3 Derive the formula for the reliability of a triplexed component.

4 Discuss the effect of preventive maintenance on system availability. [Hint: consider the reduction in availability due to maintenance against the smaller incidence of random breakdowns likely to accrue.]

5 What is the maximum transaction throughput rate for a single-disk drive handling random transactions to a single file? (*See* p. 19 for performance characteristics of different DASD units.)

6 Can money spent improving the reliability of a system also improve its throughput?

7 Discuss the effect on system throughput of increasing the number of terminals in an on-line system. [Hint: the capacity of the system (transactions/h), number of terminals and response time are all interconnected.]

8 A disk drive has to service ten references per second with an average time of 70 ms each. How many input buffers should be provided for transactions in the queue awaiting service?

9 At what level of facility utilization will a 10 per cent increase double the response time?

10 What is the effect on response time of blocking records on a random file so that there are fewer physical references to disk?

11 Introduction to database systems†

Introduction

As we have previously seen, indexed-sequential files provide a compromise between sequential files, with their capability for efficient batch processing, and direct files with their more immediate response. The fact that standard software exists for indexed-sequential files means that there is less design effort required by the user than for a direct file where the user has to choose an algorithm, loading method, overflow handling routine, etc. It is no surprise, therefore, that indexed-sequential files are widely used on all types of machine from the microcomputer to the large mainframe.

Since indexed-sequential files were first introduced, the DP environment has changed quite considerably. Perhaps the two most significant changes that affect file organization have been the move towards on-line systems and the database approach. On-line systems have produced a need for quick response to queries and a high measure of security and integrity, whereas the database approach has produced a requirement for the facility to access data records in many different ways depending on the application. It is worth noting that these two developments do not necessarily go hand in hand and that it is possible to have a database system that is not on-line and vice versa.

In this chapter, we shall examine some of the concepts of database systems as they affect the file designer. Some specific database management systems (DBMSs) will also be described and analyzed.

The database approach

With the types of file organization discussed so far, we have seen how the design of a file or set of files can be optimized to suit the individual application. With the database approach, however, files can be accessed by several different applications—in fact, the individual applications can be viewed as data channels through which data is added to or retrieved from

† Contributed by Norman Revell, Senior Tutor, The Centre for Business Systems Analysis, The City University, London

124

the database (*see* references 34, 35). The database itself may be a single file or a set of files, the important fact being that the database can be accessed by different applications in different ways. For example, a personnel file, normally accessed via a record key or payroll number for production of payslips, etc., may need to be accessed via employee skill codes for production planning purposes. The programs accessing the database may be regular production programs such as payroll, management statistics, etc., or may be of an *ad hoc* nature and run only once, especially if high-level query facilities are provided. It is thus not sensible to optimize the database for any specific single application, as this may adversely affect some other task.

Logical and physical databases

The first stage of database design is usually concerned with designing the structure of the database independently of any specific applications.

The concepts of **logical and physical** are often used to cover the case of record blocking, where the words indicate the application and device-oriented views of a block of records. The logical concept has been extended further in databases to cover the relationships between data fields or elements as well as records. Once the data fields of a database have been determined, a **logical data model** of the database can be constructed, representing the application-oriented view of the database. The **physical database** is concerned with the actual storage of data on the available peripheral devices. The mapping or conversion of the logical database on to the physical database is normally accomplished by a set of routines known as the **database management system** (DBMS). Application programs are thus separated from the physical database and can only gain access to it via the logical database. Most database users will normally use a standard proprietary DBMS, though some organizations have written their own.

The I/O operations in application programs which access the database files are special database I/O instructions that operate on a **logical database**; the DBMS then translates these into physical I/O operations (illustrated in Fig. 11.1). The objective of this approach is to keep applications independent of physical data storage so that either can be changed with minimal disturbance to the other, at least in theory. This concept is sometimes referred to as **logical data independence**. At present, there are three generally recognized data models, namely the hierarchical, network and relational. In the hierarchical model (Fig. 11.2), data fields and records are related by a **parent–child relationship** (as illustrated in the example by motor cars and their engines). It is worth noting that the hierarchy can be deeper than the simple two levels used as illustration. The

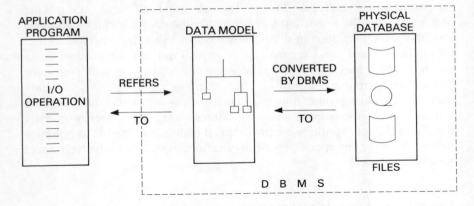

Fig. 11.1 The database environment.

network model permits a record to belong to a number of parents, thus permitting a more economical logical structure. Figure 11.3 illustrates this for the same data used in the previous example. The CODASYL database model[32] follows this structure though there are restrictions on the structures that can be built. The relational data model is entirely different in concept and is built from tables of data elements known as **relations**; thus there is no explicit structure and database operations are performed by

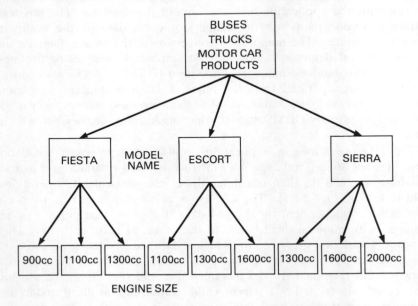

Fig. 11.2 A simple hierarchical database. (To simplify the diagram, only three of Ford's ranges of model are included.)

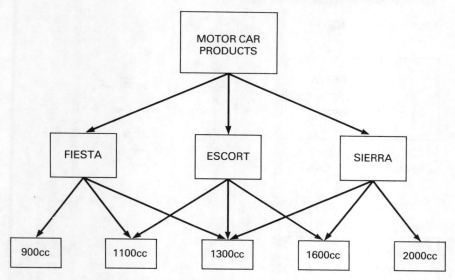

Fig. 11.3   Example of a network database.

combining relations in various ways (*see* reference 32). An example is shown in Fig. 11.4, where the car database has been broken down into two relations CAR and ENGINE. The relationships between the different models and engine options represented by the pointers in the hierarchical or network databases have to be derived from actual data values shown in the relations. In other words, there is no predefined logical structure.

The complete logical specification of a database is often referred to as the **schema** though the precise meaning of this term varies depending on implementation.

DBMS selection

In selecting a DBMS we are effectively examining a matrix of logical data models versus physical file organizations whose elements are specific DBMS products. Once a data model has been selected, a choice of the DBMSs supporting the model can be made in such a way as to optimize the performance of the physical database for a given environment. It is here that there is the first opportunity for optimization, since the database can only be constructed using the physical file organizations supported by this DBMS. For example, if an organization has large volumes of sequential batch processing and relatively few query-type applications, then choice of a DBMS based on inverted random files with multiple indices is unlikely ever to achieve the same performance as a DBMS using indexed-sequential files, however well the former is optimized.

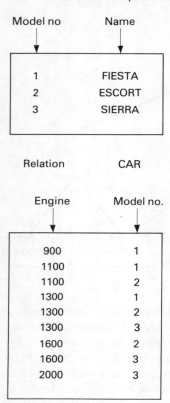

Model no   Name

1	FIESTA
2	ESCORT
3	SIERRA

Relation   CAR

Engine   Model no.

900	1
1100	1
1100	2
1300	1
1300	2
1300	3
1600	2
1600	3
2000	3

Fig. 11.4 A simple relational database.

Once all functional requirements have been met, a DBMS should be chosen which is most suited to its operational environment. The larger DBMSs normally offer scope for matching the database to any particular environment by giving a choice of physical file organizations covering the whole spectrum from pure query to large batch-type applications. Smaller systems, such as those for mini- and microcomputers, do not generally offer such a choice.

General-purpose DBMSs generally aim to be self-optimizing by using an extension of the virtual storage principle. The physical database (at its simplest level) may be viewed as a random file of database 'pages', which contain not only the stored data but pointers and indices representing the relationships between records. The DBMS attempts to keep the most frequently used pages in memory, only referencing the physical database where necessary. Such a database system can be optimized by controlling the amount of memory available, record placement, and access paths to data, the latter two being determined by the logical data model. The IDMS system offered by the Cullinane Corporation represents a good example of this.

When a database has become operational, the individual files may be optimized by the techniques appropriate to those file organizations (*see* the chapter concerned). This would normally be performed by a new function within the DP department, namely that of database administration (DBA). It is unlikely that the overall hardware performance in a database environment would equal the performance of having separate applications each carefully optimized (as early DBMS users found to their cost!) because of the overheads needed to provide the flexibility of data access; indeed, hardware performance is seldom given as a reason for the adoption of a database approach. A difficulty in optimizing the performance of a database system lies in knowing precisely what is happening to the database at any one time, especially in an on-line environment. If a log of transactions is maintained (which is normal for security and recovery purposes) and each transaction is time stamped, an analysis of the transactions may help optimization by building up an activity profile for the database. This approach would be more effective in situations where routine applications predominate rather than those in which query-type applications form a significant part of the workload, since it relies on historical data. Most DBMSs themselves will provide statistics which may be used in a similar way.

File structures in database systems

In the previous section, we saw how the choice of a logical data model and database management system (DBMS) determined the choice of file organization. In general, the closer the physical storage organization mirrors the logical data structure and processing, the better the perform-ance of the database. In this section, we shall explore the physical database organization further by studying examples of some actual DBMSs.

Use of inverted files for database systems

The concept of an inverted file was discussed in Chapter 8. If a file is fully inverted then it is possible to access it using any of its data fields as a key. Figure 11.5 shows the simple motor car database both before and after inversion. In practice, if DASDs are being used, access to the file can be provided without the need for inversion via secondary indices as shown in Fig. 11.6. Sometimes it may not be necessary to access the file via every one of its data fields, in which case indices are constructed only for those fields by which it is necessary to reference the file. This is known as **partial inversion**. An inverted file or set of linked files can thus form the basis of a

PRODUCT MODEL ENGINE

1	FIESTA	900cc
2	FIESTA	1100cc
3	FIESTA	1300cc
4	ESCORT	1100cc
5	ESCORT	1300cc
6	ESCORT	1600cc
7	SIERRA	1300cc
8	SIERRA	1600cc
9	SIERRA	2000cc

↑
KEYFIELD

INVERSION →

ATTRIBUTE PRODUCT

FIESTA	1	2	3
ESCORT	4	5	6
SIERRA	7	8	9
900cc	1		
1100cc	2	4	
1300cc	3	5	7
1600cc	6	8	
2000	9		

↑
INVERTED
KEYFIELD

Fig. 11.5 A simple inverted file.

DBMS, permitting access to the database via any specified key for which an index has been constructed. From a performance point of view, there are three major drawbacks. Firstly, all relevant indices would need updating whenever a record is added to the file; secondly, efficient batch processing is only possible in the sequence of the original file(s); and

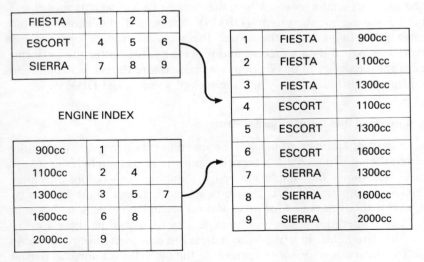

MODEL INDEX

FIESTA	1	2	3
ESCORT	4	5	6
SIERRA	7	8	9

ENGINE INDEX

900cc	1		
1100cc	2	4	
1300cc	3	5	7
1600cc	6	8	
2000cc	9		

1	FIESTA	900cc
2	FIESTA	1100cc
3	FIESTA	1300cc
4	ESCORT	1100cc
5	ESCORT	1300cc
6	ESCORT	1600cc
7	SIERRA	1300cc
8	SIERRA	1600cc
9	SIERRA	2000cc

Fig. 11.6 Use of indices for inversion.

finally, at least two references are required for each record—one to the index and one to the file itself.

A problem of this type of file structure is that it is difficult to provide efficient batch processing for more than a single application. The standardization on the CODASYL data model mentioned previously has led to the development of DBMSs which adhere to it. The IDMS system from the Cullinane Corporation, available on a wide range of mini- and mainframe systems, is a case in point. On a smaller scale, the MDBS system which runs on microcomputers and minicomputers is also based on the CODASYL model, so that databases developed on a small system can be upward compatible without the need to change the data model.

Nevertheless, for query-type database applications, an inverted file structure can work effectively, and it forms the basis of several DBMSs such as ADABAS and SYSTEM 2000. A simple example of such a DBMS is the CROMEMCO-DBMS package designed to run on the CROMEMCO range of microcomputers. This is a single-user single-file data base system. Records are added serially to the database, and indices are maintained for designated data fields (known as sort fields). These indices are maintained in sequence (as in Fig. 11.7) so that every addition to the database causes indices to be re-sequenced. The overheads caused by this constant updating of index files are quite acceptable in the personal computing environment for which this DBMS was designed, but would be less acceptable for larger scale use, e.g. with multiple users and/or larger files. The queuing formula in the previous chapter gives a means of calculating the expected terminal response times in such a case.

This type of structure, often in indexed-sequential form with secondary key indices, forms the basis for some of the smaller scale minicomputer DBMSs and relational systems, as well as the mainframe DBMSs previously mentioned.

An IMS database

IBM's Information Management System (IMS) is based on a hierarchical data model and offers the user a choice of physical file organization to suit his processing needs. The IMS packages comprise both a data communications system and a database system, though it is only the latter that we shall look at here. The building blocks of an IMS database are known as **segments** and the language for specifying their structure in the database is DL/1—data language number 1. Each segment may comprise one or more datafields, the highest level being known as the **root segment**. In the simple example we have chosen, the root segment would be the *car model* and the *engine* segment would be a *child* segment of the root segment (which is an alternative to the term *parent* segment) in the *parent–child* structure outlined in the previous section.

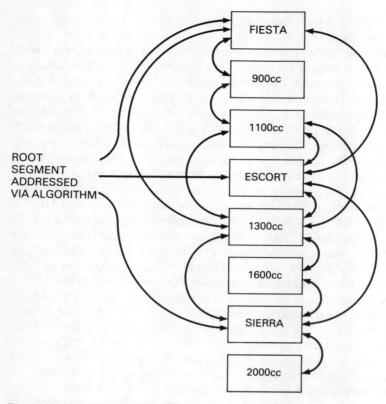

Fig. 11.7 HDAM database (IMS).

There were originally four physical file organization methods provided for an IMS database:

HSAM   Hierarchical Sequential Access Method
HISAM   Hierarchical Indexed Sequential Access Method
HDAM   Hierarchical Direct Access Method
HIDAM   Hierarchical Indexed Direct Access Method

We shall examine each of these in turn.

1. HSAM stores the database as sequential fixed-length records, each record comprising a root segment and as many subordinate segments as can be accommodated, overflow segments occupying the next physical record(s). Thus in our example there would be three records, one of each root segment of FIESTA, ESCORT, SIERRA, and the engine segments would be part of their respective parent records. This method is suitable only for batch processing of the database using either magnetic tape or DASD.

2. HISAM stores the root segment and as many lower-level segments as possible (remaining segments being held in overflow) as ISAM records. Thus it is possible to access a given root segment at random via its key and thence gain access to the lower-level segments.
3. HDAM stores all the segments separately as a chained direct file, with pointers between levels in the hierarchy and between segments at the same level. Figure 11.3 illustrates how the motor car example might appear using HDAM. There is no significance in the physical position of segments, since they are connected via pointers, though to minimize seek times it is advantageous to place segments which are normally accessed together physically close to each other. The root segment is accessed via a randomizing algorithm.
4. HIDAM is similar to HDAM but uses an ISAM file as an index to the root segment and thence to lower-level segments by chaining.

Both HDAM and HIDAM may take more storage space than the other techniques, since each segment has its associated pointers stored with it. However, the ability to access individual segments makes them suitable for on-line use where rapid response to transactions is required. HISAM (and HSAM) is more suitable for an environment where high-volume batch applications predominate. It is interesting to note that in the early versions of IMS, IBM was aware of the shortcomings of ISAM and used a special access method (OSAM) to handle overflow and also to form a basis for the segment chaining used in HDAM and HIDAM. IMS/VS now uses VSAM (*see* pp. 95–100 for a description) as a basis for HISAM, HDAM and HIDAM.

From a file design point of view, IMS illustrates well the two stages of performance optimization possible in a database environment, namely:

1. The selection of appropriate physical file organizations from those supported by the DBMS (if there is a choice).
2. The optimization of individual files by appropriate techniques (covered in previous chapters).

A CODASYL database

We shall consider here the MDBS system (*see* reference 37) as being one of the previously mentioned DBMSs which have adopted the CODASYL data model.

A CODASYL database is built from a number of different **record types** which are related using a **set** concept. The set provides for the linkage of records. In our motor car example, the set is CAR–ENGINE (*see* Fig. 11.8).

The purpose of the 'crowsfeet' pointers on Fig. 11.8 is to indicate that many car records may have a common engine record and many engine

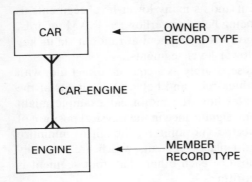

Fig. 11.8 Use of SETS.

records may belong to a common car record. This type of relationship is known as **many-to-many** and is an extension of the CODASYL specifications which only permit one-to-many relationships between two record types. The figure showing all the record types and their relationships is known as a Bachman diagram. A typical MDBS database may have 20 to 30 different record types whereas a typical IDMS database may have 80 to 90! The actual data records are stored in fixed-size pages, and are linked to each other by means of a database key which specifies an absolute page number and an offset within a page, showing where a record is to be found. This is usually completely transparent to the application program which will access records at a logical level via the set relationships.

The important design parameters are thus to select an optimal page size for the DASD being used and to ascertain that enough main storage is available to prevent **thrashing** of the database. Simplifying the database structure by having fewer SETS can sometimes improve the performance, though there is a risk that the performance may actually be *worse* due to programs having to use more indirect routes to access a given record-type on the database.

The CODASYL specifications allow for access directly to records via CALC keys, in other words the DBMS applies a randomizing algorithm to access the records of a given type. This can give a better performance if a particular record-type is a commonly used entry point to the database, for example a customer name and address record, since there is no need to access intermediate SET pointers or indices.

Revision questions

1 How would a relational and a CODASYL database system differ in the eyes of (a) an end user, (b) a programmer and (c) an analyst.

2   A manufacturer makes finished products from subassemblies which in turn are made from bought-in components. Each product may be produced in any one of a number of plants and each subassembly may be similarly produced. A product comprises one or more subassemblies. Any given part is available from a number of possible suppliers, whereas a supplier may produce one or more parts. Design a relational database for this application.

3   Design an IMS database for Question 2.

4   Design an MDBS (extended CODASYL) database for Question 2.

5   Give examples of the type of database for which you might choose HIDAM as a suitable organization in IMS.

6   Which of the record-types in Question 4 would you specify for accessing CALC keys and why?

7   Specify an initial load program (in flowchart or pseudo-code) for your solution to Question 4.

8   What types of application do *not* need a database solution?

9   How would you select a database management system for a given application?

12 Security of data files

Introduction

In this chapter, those aspects of security that can be directly influenced by the file designer are discussed. References to security in the wider sense are also given.

Data file handling will be planned to avoid errors, and to put right as quickly as possible any errors that do arise. This may be within the run itself, after the completion of a processing run, or by the use of alternative machines and data, depending on the severity of the errors that have occurred.

Database and on-line systems pose their own particular set of problems and are dealt with in a separate section. The wider aspects of security have been covered by Martin[43], and the specific precautions that can be taken by programmers are discussed in the *NCC Programming Standards*[44], and in *Keeping Computers Under Control*[42].

Avoiding read–write errors

A file held on magnetic disk is seldom corrupted due to mechanical write errors; however, extra certainty can be provided by ensuring that the information recorded on disk is the same as that held in the I/O area. This is done by issuing READ and COMPARE instructions after the WRITE. It will mean waiting an extra revolution after each write, and for that reason it adds significantly to run times.

Magnetic tapes are relatively error prone, and the read-after-write check is usually standard, using two separate read–write heads. Tapes normally re-try records that are in error.

Some more expensive modern tapes have two parity bits per character and can put right all one-bit errors and many two-bit errors **in flight**—that is, without the need to rewind and try again. If these are available, they should be used on the most important or largest files. In this way, they will minimize tape-passing time.

Restarting a run

Very long runs present a special problem. Breakdowns caused by power or mechanical failure become more likely the longer the run, and at some point it may become difficult to finish the job at all, due to its length and complexity.

Perhaps the run produces a production plan. Even if failure is unlikely it is not sufficient, on those few occasions when failure does occur, to rerun the program and give the results on Tuesday, if the plan is to start on Monday each week.

These problems can be much reduced by taking checkpoints at intervals during the run. After a failure, the run can be restarted from the last checkpoint, rather than from the start.

On magnetic tape a checkpoint system is easy to implement. Reels are backward spaced to the appropriate checkpoint record, reels that have been removed are replaced, and all processing since then is carried out once more. Magnetic disk files are more complex, as the records are updated in place. Checkpoint records have to be used to restore the files to the state they were in when the checkpoint was taken, and this may take some time.

The loss of time due to checkpoints will increase run times as shown in Fig. 12.1. For very long runs, or under difficult conditions such as intermittent power failures, the average time of a run may be reduced by using checkpoints, as shown in Fig. 12.2. It should be noted that the optimum number of checkpoints is relatively low; for a 0.2 probability of failure three or four are sufficient, and this only increases to six for the very high probability of 0.65. (This, of course, applies only to the specific run analyzed here. For any given case checkpoint, run and restart have to be analyzed. *See* reference 45.)

Probabilities of failure as high as 0.2 are not often met, so it is not often possible to reduce average run times by building in a number of

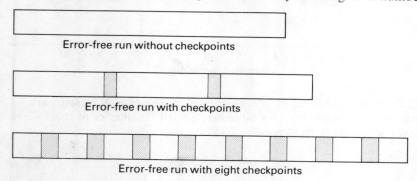

Error-free run without checkpoints

Error-free run with checkpoints

Error-free run with eight checkpoints

Fig. 12.1 Checkpoints add to the time taken by an error-free run.

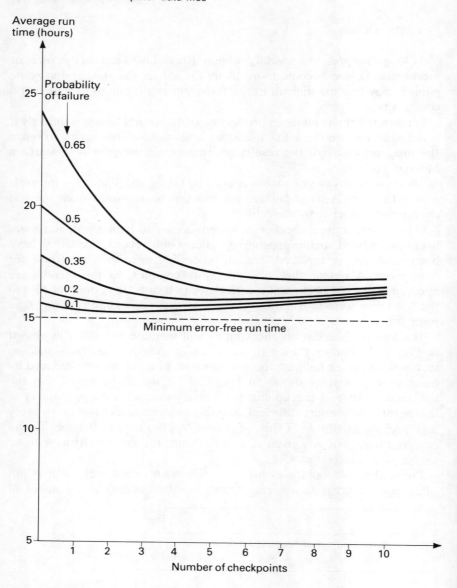

Fig. 12.2 As the probability of failure increases, the reduction in average run time achieved by checkpoints becomes more marked and the number of checkpoints that gives optimum results increases.

checkpoints. Usually, the limited time available to complete a run is the reason checkpoints are taken.

In Fig. 12.3, the overall time to complete an 8 h run is shown with one failure. The overall run time is increased by half the average time between

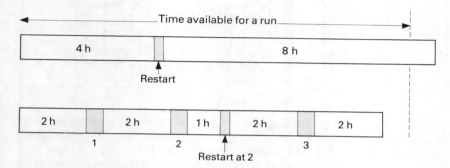

Fig. 12.3 Checkpoints reduce the overall time of a run after failure. This allows runs to be completed within a given time limit, but increases the run time of error-free runs. The top band shows the rerunning of a job without checkpoints. The lower band shows the same job being rerun with checkpoints.

checkpoints. This leads to a 12 h run if no checkpoints are taken, but a 9 h run, plus checkpoint and restart times, if three checkpoints are included.

If only 10 h are available to run the program, it would be sensible to use a number of checkpoints even if this did not give an improvement in average run time, because then the run could be completed within the 10 h limit even after a failure. If possible, allowance should be made for multiple failures[45]. (*See also* pp. 153–5.)

Repeating a run

The output from a run, or the examination of check data in file trailer labels, may show that an error has occurred. The run may have to be repeated, and if the master file has been corrupted it will first have to be recreated.

Magnetic tape back-up is usually provided by the grandfather–father–son method, sometimes extended to 20 or more generations. This is easily arranged, as updating involves the creation of a new file on each run, as shown in Fig. 12.4.

Disks cause extra problems, as updating is carried out in place. Files have to be dumped to tape at intervals and restored to disk when necessary to recreate the file. This is shown in Fig. 12.5.

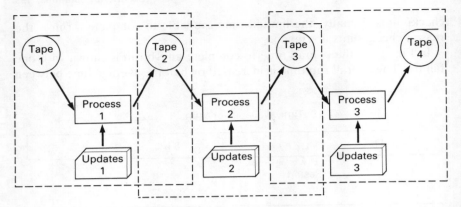

Fig. 12.4 Tape security. The updating of tape files calls for the rewriting of the file on a new tape reel. As each run is completed without error, the old tape and the updates are retained. If Tape 2 is subsequently corrupted, Tape 1 and Update 1 can be used to recreate Tape 2. The minimum number of tapes required is three; this is referred to as the grandfather–father–son method.

Recovering from disaster

Fire, bombs, earthquakes, etc., provide a challenge to the designer. Not only the data file, but also the hardware may be lost. In this case, recovery depends on:

1. The availability of a compatible machine. This means that a CPU large enough to hold the program, compatible devices, the same operating system and all necessary special features must be available. Some companies have identical installations in several centres, giving automatic back-up. Smaller companies will have to find as close a fit as possible among other users. Often this means that one partner is fully backed up, while the other can only run programs that require a limited set of facilities on the installation available. The system designer should seek for as high a degree of compatibility as possible in looking for a back-up partner.
2. The availability of data. Copies of files and updates will have to be stored at a distance, preferably in different buildings, and renewed regularly. The use of fireproof cabinets in the computer room gives some security, but not sufficient to ensure the ability to recreate the operations of an installation in all circumstances.

Security in on-line and database systems

In this section, we shall look at some of the problems of file security in on-line and database systems which are unique to those systems. In the

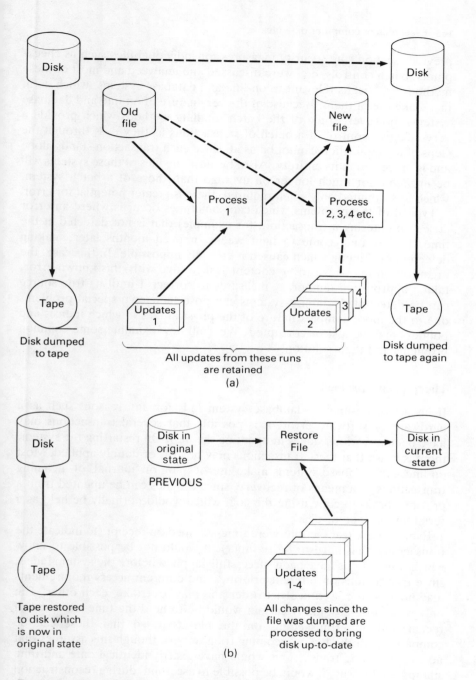

Fig. 12.5 As a security precaution, disk files are dumped to tape at intervals. This process is shown in (a). When the disk is dumped to tape again the updates since the first dump, and the tapes used for it, can be released. Diagram (b) shows the procedure after a failure.

previous section, the security measures for individual files such as check-points, batch controls, etc. were discussed and analyzed and most of these methods are just as relevant to on-line and database systems, which do in fact make use of them. Because of the very nature of on-line and database systems, however, some of the batch totalling methods which provide a very effective control of a batch of transactions as they pass through the steps of an application cannot be used, since each transaction stands alone and is processed in its entirety. Also, because the files of these systems will be *available* for much longer on average than those of a batch system, which are mounted only when required, there is greater potential for error.

Typical of the problems which can sometimes occur is where an error arises (in entering a transaction, for example) that is not detected at the time. It may only come to light weeks or even months later, making detection of the bug which caused it virtually impossible. In this case, the organization may have to be content just to 'live with' this known error, taking appropriate temporary measures to correct it until its true source can be detected. Database systems can pose their own special problems due to the more complex nature of the physical files in which indices and pointers may be lost or corrupted. We shall now examine some common problems and their solutions.

The 'pipeline' problem

If an active on-line or database system fails for any reason, such as a hardware or software error, it is possible that several transactions may have been at various stages in updating the files. On restarting the system, there is a risk that these transactions may be lost, or doubly applied. Most on-line and database systems make use of a log or 'journal' of incoming transactions as a means of recovery, since the files can be updated from a previous back-up copy using this log, which would normally be held as a serial file on tape or disk.

Even if these transactions were time-stamped on receipt (to indicate the transactions that have to be re-input), it would not be possible to know which transactions have been successfully applied before the system failed, since transactions of different priorities and different access requirements may not be processed in strict order and may 'overtake' each other. The only way to be absolutely certain would be to hold the time-stamp of all recent updating transactions on the file itself, so that these can be compared with the log of incoming transactions, though this assumes that no two incoming transactions would have exactly identical date and time stamps. In this way, it would be possible to ascertain, during reconstruction of the files, which transactions had been successfully applied.

A variation of this method is to use a serial number for each incoming transaction and to keep an additional log of successful file update transactions, though this approach has the overhead of an additional file reference. The overhead of logging transactions can be reduced by blocking the log files, though to a large extent this may negate their purpose, since several transaction log records may be lost in the output buffer in the course of a system failure.

There can be a problem with some database management systems that make use of the 'paging' principle for efficient processing. Pages which have been changed—by the addition of new records, for example—only get written back to the physical database when storage requirements demand it, or when the database is closed. Thus, even a transaction log may not always be reliable. A useful facility which many databases possess is a **forced write**, whereby a write transaction is immediately applied to the database. An alternative is a utility command to **flush** the buffers periodically, forcing all database pages of records that have been modified to be rewritten to the database. This latter method can cause quite serious overheads and therefore a trade-off needs to be made between security and performance.

A method used by some database systems to avoid problems of system failure during complex transactions is to defer the physical updating of the database until the transaction has completed, thereby maintaining the integrity of the physical database. This method is sometimes called **page image** posting and is shown in greater detail in Fig. 12.6. Pages get written to a temporary file while the transaction is executing and at the end get copied on to the database. Any hardware or software failure while the transaction is executing will not affect the database.

Record locking

In on-line and database systems, a problem to be avoided is the **deadly embrace**, where two or more transactions are attempting to access the

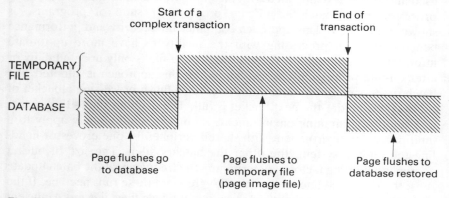

Fig. 12.6 Page image posting.

same physical record. In order to avoid this, techniques known collectively as **record locking** need to be employed which limit simultaneous access to a record. These techniques are also useful to maintain the integrity of the file or database. For example, a transaction which updates a stock file with new stock should be applied before sales transactions which may debit the stock record. In particular, for database systems it is possible to define two locking mechanisms.

Active locking is where a transaction has to specify which records and access paths it wishes to lock, and is also responsible for freeing them afterwards. **Passive locking** is where *all* records and access paths are made exclusive to a transaction automatically. This latter heavy-handed approach causes serious performance degradation in systems with a large number of users since a relatively small number of transactions could 'saturate' the database and lock out other transactions, thereby giving a poor terminal response time.

The bucket method

In many systems, update transactions are not applied immediately but are instead stored in serial files, known as buckets, for later batch updating. This is normally done for reasons of security and performance (*see* Chapters 1–3) though, of course, the major disadvantage of this approach is that query transactions will obtain an out-of-date answer. An example of this method is found in banking, where any queries concerning account balance refer to the figure that applied at the close of business the previous day, when all the update transactions were last consolidated on to the master file. Though this approach is acceptable in some applications, in others such as airline reservations—it is clearly not, and an immediate update is required.

Between these extremes a situation is possible where two buckets are used and as one is being filled with incoming transactions the other is being processed by a batch-file update program or suite of programs, as shown in Fig. 12.7. This approach combines the security and performance benefits of batch processing with the facility to have more up-to-date information on file than is the case where the file is only updated daily or after on-line processing has ceased. When this approach is adopted, the batch processing system must be designed to finish processing a bucket of transactions before the next bucket is full. The diagram shows this system in a multiprogramming environment, though it could equally apply to a multiprocessor environment with shared peripherals, one processor handling the on-line system, the other the batch system. The size of bucket chosen is a limiting factor in determining the frequency of the batch update runs; the larger the bucket size, the less frequent these runs need be. If the update run involves sequential processing of whole files, it is more efficient

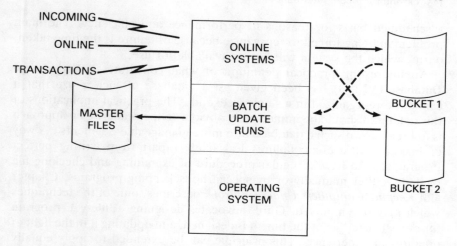

Fig. 12.7 The operation of the bucket system for updating an on-line database in batch mode (for greater throughput).

to have fewer runs, each containing more updates—and so a higher hit-rate—than if skip sequential or random processing is involved.

The control of access via software

In most on-line and database systems, there will be control of access to files via security codes (*see* references 42, 43). This is often at two levels: first a sign-on code, and second passwords for certain files or parts of the database. In an on-line environment, it is possible to link the two together by having different classes of user (identified by a sign-on code) who may have different levels of access. For example, some users may only be allowed to query parts of the files or database, while others are allowed to update or add new records. This can be very useful for training purposes where a special 'trainee' log code can cause the system to simulate the appropriate response while taking no action. If a CODASYL-based DBMS is being used then there is scope for security control via the SUB-SCHEMA, each user program being given its own subset of the entire database which it is allowed to process.

'Catastrophic' file and database failures

These are defined as failures where it is impossible to continue processing by going back to a previous version of the files and applying the transactions again, as previously described. Any system, from a single random or indexed file to a complex database, may be rebuilt from a serial dump of the records, and indeed this reorganization is often performed on a scheduled basis for reasons of performance and efficiency. The main problem in being forced to reorganize because of failure is the time taken, during which the system will not be available for use.

An interesting practical definition of what constitutes a **Very Large Database** (VLDB) has been given as 'a database of such a size that it cannot be reorganized in a single weekend'. The practical implications of this definition should be immediately obvious to the reader! One approach is to break down such a database into more manageable 'segments'. A way of making catastrophic failures less likely (apart from writing perfect programs) is to have a regular procedure of examining and checking file contents either manually or by special housekeeping programs. Chapter 4 of *Keeping Computers Under Control*[42] describes some of the techniques which may be employed. Gilb[40] advocates designing a 'file-vet' program for every master file at the time it is designed, and updating it in the light of operational experience. This principle can be extended to apply equally well to database systems, and reduce the likelihood that a number of 'soft' errors can conspire over time to produce a 'catastrophic' failure.

Conclusion

In summary, the problems of on-line and database systems are twofold on account of (a) greater immediacy of response and (b) more complex transaction processing. All security methods affect system performance and therefore a trade-off usually needs to be made between level of security and performance. Moreover, the costs of providing greater security are more marked than the marginal costs of providing them for batch systems.

Total security is not achievable, and the user has to decide what level is acceptable for a given application. While extra cost will buy more security, nothing is more effective in eliminating error than careful analysis of the problem. Expenditure on hardware for security purposes should always *follow* design, rather than *precede* it.

Revision questions

1   Distinguish between data security and the wider aspects of security.

2   What are the sources of data errors that are known to you?

3   How are data errors during reading or writing guarded against in (a) disk handling and (b) tape handling?

4   When might a run be restarted from some point other than the beginning? How do tape and disk differ in the difficulty of doing this?

5 Explain the two main economic reasons for using checkpoints, comparing and contrasting them.

6 How can a system be protected against total disaster, e.g. earthquakes, bombs, etc?

7 Why—if at all—should a system *not* give 100 per cent protection against loss of data?

8 Describe the grandfather–father–son method of protecting tape systems.

9 Describe the dump-restore method of protecting disk-based systems.

10 How would you ensure data security in a system without tapes or removable disks?

11 Are CODASYL databases easier to protect than relational ones?

12 How would you arrange for the recovery of a database where the access paths (indices, pointers, etc.) but *not* the actual data had been corrupted.

13 Following the previous question flowchart a dump/reload program for a CODASYL database.

14 What are the advantages and disadvantages of holding each relation in a relational database as a separate physical file?

15 Discuss the security advantages of distributing a large on-line application over several physical sites, rather than at one central site.

13 Case studies in file design

Introduction

In most cases, the designer will be in no doubt that a particular file organization will be required, and the design process becomes one of optimization only. Guidance in these cases can usually be found in Chapter 2 on choice of file organization—to confirm the choice—and the appropriate chapter to optimize the selected design.

Three cases are examined in this chapter to show the sequence of calculations that is followed when the designer is in doubt about any given decision. (A fourth case is also briefly considered.) Although these cases do not cover every possibility, the reader will be able to check on the usage of most of the techniques described here. Together with the examples given in the rest of the text, all the more common situations are covered.

1. Tape blocking

An example of the calculations involved in arriving at optimum blocking factors for a magnetic tape file was given on pp. 37 and 43. The case examined here is rather more complicated, but often arises.

When a file is used by more than one program, the optimum for each of the programs can be calculated separately, but after this the blocking factor chosen has to be the *least* of the various figures calculated for each program. All other programs will have to be handled by a sub-optimization, re-allocating the space made available by the reduced blocking factor required for the shared file.

Assume that the two programs, A and B, use the following files:

Program A

File 1 (Input Customer)	100 000 records of 475 characters, double buffered
File 2 (Output Customer)	100 000 records of 475 characters, double buffered
File 3 (Stock)	15 000 records of 250 characters, double buffered

File 4 (Update Invoice)   5000 records of 45 characters, single buffered

File 5 (Print Invoice)   5000 records of 120 characters, single buffered

20 000 characters of storage are available to program A for I/O areas. As a result, the theoretical optima can be calculated as was shown on pp. 44–5:

1. $\sqrt{100\,000 \times 475 \times 2}$ =   9 746.79

     $+ \sqrt{100\,000 \times 475 \times 2}$ =   9 746.79

     $+ \sqrt{15\,000 \times 250 \times 2}$ =   2 738.61

     $+ \sqrt{5000 \times 45}$ =   474.34

     $+ \sqrt{5000 \times 120}$ =   774.60

     $= \Sigma \sqrt{R_i D_i C_i}$ = 23 481.14

2.   Divide by S =   1.1741

3.   Invert   =   0.85175

4.   Store result

5/6. Calculate $R_i/C_i D_i$ and take square root

     $\sqrt{100\,000/(475 \times 2)}$ = 10.2597

7.   Multiply by stored result $B_1 = B_2 = 8.74$

Repeat steps 5–7 for three remaining $R_i/C_i D_i$ ($i = 3, 4, 5$):

5/6. $\sqrt{15\,000/(250 \times 2)}$ =   5.4772

7. $B_3 = 4.67$

5/6. $\sqrt{5000/45}$ = 10.5409

7. $B_4 = 8.98$

5/6. $\sqrt{5000/120}$ =   6.4550

7. $B_5 = 5.50$

As a first check on the accuracy of this calculation, it is *essential* to ensure that the calculated blocks fit—and fill—20 000 storage positions.

File 1 requires $2 \times 8.74 \times 475 = 8303$ characters
File 2 requires $2 \times 8.74 \times 475 = 8303$ characters
File 3 requires $2 \times 4.67 \times 250 = 2335$ characters
File 4 requires $1 \times 8.98 \times 45 \ = \ 404$ characters
File 5 requires $1 \times 5.50 \times 120 = \ 660$ characters
Total storage space required $= 20005$ characters

Given the approximation to three significant figures because the final results must be integers, this is acceptably close to 20 000.

At this stage a 'trial' solution is required. As a check on this solution, we should first calculate the 'optimum' solution:

Total number of IBGs is

$$\frac{100\ 000}{8.74} + \frac{100\ 000}{8.74} + \frac{15\ 000}{4.67} + \frac{5000}{8.98} + \frac{5000}{5.50} = 27\ 563 \quad \text{(rounded up)}$$

Table 13.1 shows the results for a series of trial solutions, the best of which gives 27 780 IBGs. This result, like the optimum, is rounded up for each value, since part blocks count as a full block.

Table 13.1 Theoretical and integer solutions for possible blocking factors for program A. The optimum integer solution is asterisked.

Comment	B_1	B_2	B_3	B_4	B_5	Total IBGs
Optimum	8.74,8.74	8.74,8.74	4.67,4.67	8.98	5.50	27 563
Assume B_1 and $B_2 = 9$,	9,9	9,9	3.96,3.96	7.67	4.69	27 731
	9,9	9,9	4,4	12	3	28 058
	9,9	9,9	4,4	9	4	27 780*
Sub-optimum trials	9,9	9,9	4,4	6	5	27 808
Check $B_3 = 5$	9,9	9,9	5,5	4	2	28 974
Assume B_1 and $B_2 = 8$,	8,8	8,8	6.56,6.56	12.69	7.77	28 326

As the sub-optimum for which $B_1 = B_2 = 8$ is less beneficial than three of the integer solutions for which $B_1 = B_2 = 9$, no further searching is necessary. The optimum integer solution is asterisked.

As a final check on the correctness of this solution, ensure that it takes up no more than 20 000 storage positions.

(9,9), (9,9), (4,4), 9,4 is the solution
$4 \times 9 \times 475 + 2 \times 4 \times 250 + 9 \times 45 + 4 \times 120 = 19\,985$

Hence, the solution is a possible one.

Note: a solution that is 'better' than this can easily be achieved by altering the limit of 20 000 storage positions; although this may be possible in an actual situation, it is not an acceptable solution to this problem.

In an update run that changes the stock file to reflect recent additions, deletions and alterations, the file arrangements might be as follows.

Program B:

File 3 (Stock)	15 000 records of 250 characters, double buffered (as before)
File 6 (Update Stock)	750 records of 250 characters, single buffered
File 7 (Print Log)	1000 records of 325 characters, double buffered

In this case, additions, deletions and both old and new versions of altered records are stored in the log file for later printout. Assume that this program has 12 000 positions available for input–output. The optimum and best integer solutions can be calculated following the same procedure as before; the results are given in Table 13.2.

Table 13.2 Calculation of the optimum integer solution for program B. It is asterisked.

Remarks	B_3	B_6	B_7	Total IBGs
Theoretical optimum	16.52,16.52	5.23	3.74,3.74	1320
Trial 1 $B_3 = 18$	18,18	4	3,3	1356
Trial 2 $B_3 = 17$	17,17	6	3,3	1342
	17,17	3	4,4	1383
Trial 3 $B_3 = 16$	16,16	8	3,3	1366
	16,16	5	4,4	1338*
	16,16	2	5,5	1513
Trial 4 $B_3 = 15$	15,15	7	4,4	1358
	15,15	5	5,5	1350
	15,15	3	6,6	1417

Comparing the two solutions, it seems likely that the conditions for Program B should be suboptimized, rather than those for Program A. This proves to be the case, as is shown in Table 13.3.

Table 13.3 Possible integer solutions for programs A and B with File 3 shared. A blocking factor of 4 for File 3 is optimal.

Remarks	B_1	B_2	B_3	B_4	B_5	B_6	B_7	Total IBGs
Program A	9,9	9,9	4,4	9	4			27 780
Program B			4,4			14	10,10	3 904
Overall								31 684
Program A	6,6	6,6	16,16	5	3			36 939
Program B			16,16			5	4,4	1 338
Overall								38 277

The best way to block the records in file B, to take account of the needs of both Program A and Program B, is thus in four record blocks.

2. Indexed sequential or sequential?

Generally, this question will be answered by referring to p. 87. On occasions, however, it may not be so straightforward.

Consider a file for which the last ten update runs have referenced the following percentages of records:

2.37, 3.84, 7.26, 4.87, 4.91, 6.31, 5.08, 5.55, 9.12, 6.09.

If there is any direct access, that would tilt the decision in favour of an indexed sequential organization. Assume that there is not. In that case, the analysis runs as follows.

The ten runs give an average hit rate of 5.54 per cent. If this were to be maintained, it would be possible to decide on a file organization for the foreseeable future. However, the figures look as if they are part of a trend rather than typical variations about the average of 5.54 per cent. A regression analysis shows that this is the case, and that the expected hit rate for run n will be given by

$$\text{hit-rate} = 3.41 + 0.39n \qquad (13.1)$$

This gives us a measure of the rate of growth of file activity.

As ten records per track are stored in the indexed-sequentially organized file, an estimate of the expected number of tracks that will *not* be hit is given by the expression

$$\text{non-hit track \%} = 100 \times \exp\left(-10 \times \text{hit rate}\right) \qquad (13.2)$$

This gives the figures in Table 13.4 for a number of hit-rate percentages.

Table 13.4 Tracks not hit, depending on hit-rate.

Hit-rate %	Tracks not hit %
2.37	79.0
5.54	57.5
9.12	40.2
10.50	35.0

The hit-rates chosen are the lowest, average and highest given in the original data, and the break-even percentage between sequential and indexed sequential file organization. From Equation (13.1), it will occur on run 19 if the trend *is* a straight line and *does* continue.

As the analyst has a further nine runs in hand before the file should be reorganized as a sequential file, it would be advisable to collect as much other data on the file as possible before run 19 is reached. In particular, any seasonal or unusual influences on file activity (e.g. increased demand due to a local or national advertising campaign) should be looked out for. In their absence, the file should be reorganized at a convenient time following run 18. For general guidance in this area, see reference 26.

3. Use of checkpoints in a specific case

Assume that a program which takes 4 h to run fails on average once in every three runs due to some problem such as device, CPU or power failure. Each checkpoint added takes 10 min to record, while restarting the run takes 5 min.

Faced with these figures, the designer would have to decide on the number of checkpoints, if any, to build into the run in order to save time overall.

It is worth noting that such a high probability of run failure as one in three is only likely in unusual circumstances, such as a stormy or rainy season in tropical countries, or during times of industrial unrest. For this reason, the designer should also be able to answer the *different* question of how best to meet a deadline, which is the usual reason for adding checkpoints to a run. In this case assume that the deadline is 5 h 45 min.

To answer the first question we proceed as follows. Calculate the *average* time required for the run, depending on the number of checkpoints provided. The lowest average run time indicates the optimum number of checkpoints, not allowing for multiple failures (figures for multiple failures are given in the last column in Table 13.5).

Table 13.5 Calculations leading to average run times for varying numbers of checkpoints.

Checkpoints	Runs (h)	Reruns (h)	Average time Single rerun	Multiple reruns
0	4,4,4	$2 + \frac{1}{12}$	4.69	5.00
1	$4\frac{1}{6},4\frac{1}{6},4\frac{1}{6}$	$1 + \frac{1}{12}$	4.53	4.75
2	$4\frac{1}{3},4\frac{1}{3},4\frac{1}{3}$	$\frac{2}{3} + \frac{1}{12}$	4.58	4.83
4	$4\frac{2}{3},4\frac{2}{3},4\frac{2}{3}$	$\frac{4}{10} + \frac{1}{12}$	4.84	5.22

Reruns are assumed to be necessary after *half* the original run is complete. Hence the timings in the *Reruns* column.

Looking at Table 13.5, the assumption is that failure occurs in the middle of the run, or part of a run, between checkpoints. On this basis, a single checkpoint is optimal for both *single* failures, and *multiple* failures. In order to minimize run time then, we need to work on *single* failures only.

In order to meet a deadline, we have to assume that the program fails at the *end* of a run. Multiple failures are taken into account in the figures given in the final column of Table 13.6. Results of the calculations are as given in the table.

From Table 13.6 it is clear that we cannot guarantee the run will be finished in 5 h 45 min after multiple failures, but two, three, four or five checkpoints will ensure that a single failure does not cause the deadline to

Table 13.6 Calculations leading to run times in meeting a deadline for various numbers of checkpoints.

Checkpoints	Runs (h)	Reruns (h)	Total time Single rerun	Total time Multiple reruns
0	4	$4\frac{1}{12}$	8.08	10.125
1	$4\frac{1}{6}$	$2\frac{1}{12}$	6.25	7.29
2	$4\frac{1}{3}$	$1\frac{5}{12}$	5.75	6.46
3	$4\frac{1}{2}$	$1\frac{1}{12}$	5.583	6.125
4	$4\frac{2}{3}$	$\frac{49}{60}$	5.55	5.89
5	$4\frac{5}{6}$	$\frac{3}{4}$	5.583	5.96

be missed. *No* arrangement of checkpoints can avoid multiple failures causing a problem, but on a number of assumptions given in reference 47 we can make a reasonable attempt to avoid them. Here, four checkpoints provide the best cover.

Calculation of the optimum number of checkpoints can usually be carried out as follows where α = overall run time, T = run time without failure, p = probability of failure, n = number of checkpoints and t = checkpoint time:

$$\alpha = T + \frac{Tp}{2(n + 1)(1 - p)} + nt \tag{13.3}$$

Therefore

$$\frac{d\alpha}{dn} = - \frac{Tp}{2(n + 1)^2(1 - p)} + t$$

But for an optimum, $d\alpha/dn = 0$. Therefore

$$t = \frac{Tp}{2(n + 1)^2(1 - p)}$$

From which

$$(n + 1)^2 = \frac{Tp}{2t(1 - p)}$$

which gives

$$n = \sqrt{\frac{Tp}{2t(1 - p)}} - 1 \tag{13.4}$$

For $T = 4$, $p = \frac{1}{3}$, $t = \frac{1}{6}$

$$n = \sqrt{6} - 1$$
$$= 1.45 \text{ checkpoints}$$

As in the case of blocking factors, the nearest integer is usually the best solution available. It is so in this case.

4. Direct or indexed sequential?

The guidance offered in Chapters 6 and 7 should be sufficient here, but the subject has been covered in very great detail in reference 28, for readers who require more information.

Conclusion

Using these examples and those in the text as patterns, users should be able to make their own calculations on design problems that they encounter. It is useful to try one of the worked examples without looking at the solution, in order to check whether the method is clear. In this way, it is possible to use these examples twice over, to be certain a method is understood.

Revision questions

1   What questions would you ask in deciding whether a file should be organized using the indexed-sequential or direct organization techniques? Trace the process of deciding between these techniques in the following case. (Where possible, justify your choices numerically.)

Batches of 2000 updates are received in the post daily, for a file that will take up 100 cylinders, each containing 20 tracks, independent of the file organization. Over this area of the device, the following figures apply:

minimum head movement	10 ms
average head movement	30 ms
maximum head movement	55 ms
disk rotation time	$16\frac{2}{3}$ ms

If the file is organized in IS form, one track per cylinder is set aside for overflow, and $\frac{3}{4}$ of a track for the track index.

2   In an installation that has only magnetic tapes, the customer file is used in two separate processes, the first to create invoices, and the second to prepare stock reports. Details of the files are as follows.

Invoice run:

customer file	150 000 records of 650 characters
update file	3500 records of 175 characters
print file	3500 records of 120 characters
log file	3500 records of 945 characters

Stock report run:

customer file	150 000 records of 650 characters
stock file	830 000 records of 280 characters
print file	550 000 records of 120 characters

All files will be single buffered, and 32 000 positions of storage are available for file handling.

Recommend optimum integer blocking factors for every file in the two runs. Show all your working, and trace the way you came to your decision.

3. You have been provided with an IBM 3350 disk drive, with the following characteristics;

Seek time; Minimum   10 ms
           average   25 ms
           maximum   50 ms
Data transfer rate   1.198 mb
Rotation time   16.7 ms

You are to create a file of 400 000 records, each of 400 bytes, on this disk. You know that occasional sequential printouts are required, from an off-line printer. The main function of the file is to keep up-to-date stock records of your goods. The number of daily changes—all received in the morning—have been as follows in the last twelve days.

additions	350, 297, 401, 363, 291, 344, 388, 419, 373, 500, 423, 352
deletions	304, 337, 295, 351, 287, 253, 340, 308, 269, 295, 399, 247
references	403, 519, 387, 451, 444, 372, 500, 413, 462, 390, 379, 428

Work through the process you would carry out to decide on a file organization, blocking factor and updating procedure for the daily updates. Refer to Table 13.7.

4   What happens when additions are made to an access frequency-loaded file? Does this lead to any particular action being advised by the file designer? Illustrate your answer by considering additions to the file below that will increase it to 100 per cent packing. You may assume the following figures:

packing density	15	16	17	18	19	20	75	80	85	90	95	100
percent synonyms	7.14	7.59	8.04	8.48	8.93	9.37	29.65	31.17	32.64	34.06	35.45	36.79

Explain how you would set up and process a direct file. Use COBOL instructions wherever possible to demonstrate each step. Specify the machine for which you are writing. When and how would access frequency loading improve the performance of a direct file? Demonstrate your understanding of any improvement by calculating the improvement you would expect, if any, for a file that is 75 per cent packed, and for which 20 per cent of the records give rise to 80 per cent of the accesses. Records are unblocked.

5   The file designer is often uncertain whether to batch and sort updates to an indexed-sequential file, or to process them without sorting. The number of accesses to an indexed-sequential file have been 185, 230, 250, 330, 283, 354. On the basis of

these figures, or otherwise, calculate whether it is best to batch and sort, or to process the updates directly.

Assume the following. The file takes up a complete disk, of average head movement time 30 ms, minimum head movement time 10 ms (to an adjacent track) and track rotation time of 16.7 ms. The file is organized using IBM software.

Make the decision between batching and sorting updates to this file or processing them without sorting under the following conditions: (1) the cylinder index in main storage; (2) the cylinder index on the same disk as the main file. Make each decision for (a) a sort time of zero; (b) a sort time of 1 min.

6   A particular file, holding customer account details on magnetic tape, is used in two separate runs. The first updates the customer account details, and is run daily. The second prints out selected account details, matching them against the previous month's selected records and adding a few more as requested by management. All files are on magnetic tape. Calculate the blocking factors that will minimize tape passing time for the two runs.

Run 1:
File A   3 500 000 records of 650 characters, double buffered
File B   750 000 records of   30 characters, single buffered
File C   750 000 records of 680 characters, single buffered
File D   750 000 records of 120 characters, single buffered

Space available for input–output is 31 750 characters.

Run 2:
File A   3 500 000 records of 650 characters, double buffered
File E   20 000 records of 730 characters, single buffered
File F   5000 records of   50 characters, single buffered
File G   25 000 records of 120 characters, single buffered

All the tapes in the installation are IBM 3420.8s with a data transfer rate of 1.25 million characters per second, 6250 characters to the inch, an inter-block gap of 0.3 in, and an IBG time of 1.5 ms.

7   Describe the structure and mode of operation of an indexed-sequential file, explaining carefully the considerations you would take into account in the design process. Decide how the following file will be stored and processed.

A file of 17 500 000 records is to be stored in indexed-sequential form. The records are 380 bytes in length, including keys. The hit rate is 2 per cent on sequential runs, which are required daily. At all other times the file is on-line for enquiries.

The installation has 100 removable single-density 3330 disks, that transfer data at 806 kb/s, have a single cylinder seek time of 10 ms, an average of 30 ms and a maximum of 55 ms. Rotation time is 16.67 ms.

Sixteen spindles of 3380 disk storage have just been installed. These spindles each have 885 cylinders with a maximum capacity of 712 140 bytes per cylinder. These disks have an average head movement time of 16 ms, and a minimum of 6 ms. Data is transferred at 3 Mb/s and the rotation time is 16.67 ms. *See* Table 2.2 for details of blocking on the 3330 and 3380.

Table 13.7 The relationships between number of blocks per track and the total data stored on an IBM 3350 track

Bytes per record				Number of records per track
Without keys		With keys		
Min	Max	Min	Max	
9 443	19 069	9 361	18 987	1
6 234	9 442	6 152	9 360	2
4 629	6 233	4 547	6 151	3
3 666	4 628	3 584	4 546	4
3 025	3 665	2 943	3 583	5
2 566	3 024	2 484	2 942	6
2 222	2 565	2 140	2 483	7
1 955	2 221	1 873	2 139	8
1 741	1 954	1 659	1 872	9
1 566	1 740	1 484	1 658	10
1 420	1 565	1 338	1 483	11
1 297	1 419	1 215	1 337	12
1 191	1 296	1 109	1 214	13
1 099	1 190	1 017	1 108	14
1 019	1 098	937	1 016	15
948	1 018	866	936	16
885	947	803	865	17
829	884	747	802	18
778	828	696	746	19
732	777	650	695	20
691	731	609	649	21
653	690	571	608	22
618	652	536	570	23

Bytes per record				Number of records per track
Without keys		With keys		
Min	Max	Min	Max	
186	192	104	110	51
179	185	97	103	52
172	178	90	96	53
166	171	84	89	54
159	165	77	83	55
153	158	71	76	56
147	152	65	70	57
142	146	60	64	58
136	141	54	59	59
131	135	49	53	60
126	130	44	48	61
121	125	39	43	62
116	120	34	33	63
112	115	30	33	64
107	111	25	29	65
103	106	21	24	66
99	102	17	20	67
95	98	13	16	68
91	94	9	12	69
87	90	5	8	70
83	86	4	4	71
79	82			72
76	78			73

586	617	504	535	24	72	75	74
556	585	474	503	25	69	71	75
529	555	447	473	26	66	68	76
503	528	421	446	27	62	65	77
479	502	397	420	28	59	61	78
457	478	375	396	29	56	58	79
437	456	355	374	30	53	55	80
417	436	335	354	31	50	52	81
399	416	317	334	32	47	49	82
382	398	300	316	33	45	46	83
366	381	284	299	34	42	44	84
350	365	268	283	35	39	41	85
336	349	254	267	36	37	38	86
322	335	240	253	37	34	36	87
309	321	227	239	38	32	33	88
297	308	215	226	39	29	31	89
285	296	203	214	40	27	28	90
274	284	192	202	41	25	26	91
263	273	181	191	42	23	24	92
253	262	171	180	43	20	22	93
243	252	161	170	44	18	19	94
234	242	152	160	45	16	17	95
225	233	143	151	46	14	15	96
217	224	135	142	47	12	13	97
208	216	126	134	48	10	11	98
201	207	119	125	49	8	9	99
193	200	111	118	50	6	7	100
					4	5	101
					2	3	102
					1	1	103

14 Review of the literature

The original sources of information cited in the text are briefly reviewed, together with several other key sources. They are divided into ten subject areas. The reference number sequence is the same as that used in the text, and the references are listed on pp. 165–7.

General

Owen Hanson's *Design of Computer Data Files*[1] is intended to act both as a reference and learning text. It contains a great deal of tabular information to aid design decisions and a full discussion of the factors involved in the choice and design of files. It is the natural follow-up to the present book.

Record format and handling

Walker ('Optimization of Tape Operations'[2]) and Waters ('Blocking Sequentially Processed Magnetic Files'[3]) cover the derivation of theoretical optimum blocking factors on magnetic tape. In practice, an integer solution is required, as blocks of some such figure as 6.38 records are not generally feasible—although Inglis and Dee discuss the possibility of handling part-blocks in 'Flexibility of Block-length for Magnetic Files'[4].

Walker[2] and Edwards ('Choice of Block Sizes for Magnetic Tape Files'[5]) give programs to calculate the optimum blocking factors for any given situation, Walker in FORTRAN, and Edwards in ALGOL. (This last provides the optimum *integer* solution.) Kouvatsos and Wong[6] have carried out work on this area recently (October 1983) and have provided optimizing programs in the case of variable partition size computer systems.

Sequential files

Sectioning of magnetic tape files is discussed in Owen Hanson's *Basic File Design*[7]. In his 1980 ADV Kongress paper, 'The Choice between Magnetic Tape and Magnetic Disc for Sequential Files', Owen Hanson[8] provides the detail on which the analysis given in the present book is based. Also of considerable assistance is Owen Hanson's CUBS Working Paper 'Statistical Searching of Sequential Disc Files'[9]. Figures comparing disk and tape performance are given in Ansari's MSc thesis, *Performance Evaluation of ICL Disk EDS60 using Sequential File Organization*[10].

Direct files

Addressing algorithms have been discussed by many writers. The most important contributions are 'Addressing for Random Access Storage' by Petersen[11], and 'File Organization and Addressing' by Buchholz[12]. These two papers review the whole field as it existed two decades ago, and are regarded as classics. Lum, Yuen and Dodd ('Key-to-Address Techniques: a Fundamental Performance Study on Large Existing Formatted Files'[13]) investigated randomization applied to eight large files. Kaimann, in *Structured Information Files*[14], got rather different results in examining a single large file used in hospital administration. In 'A Practitioner's Guide to Addressing Algorithms', Severance and Duhne[15] look at the whole field of algorithms once more. The results of these studies differ, and they have been assessed and used in the present book to give an overall view of randomization.

Many of the same references examine methods of minimizing the effect of synonyms once a suitable algorithm has been chosen. Other sources in this area are: 'Handling Overflows in Direct Files' by Owen Hanson[16]; *An Evaluation of the Various Parameters affecting the Design of Direct Access Files, using Descriptive, Analytical and Simulation Methods* by Yaffe[17], in which he discusses one-pass versus two-pass loading; 'Note on Random Addressing Techniques' by Heising[18]; 'Algorithms and Performance Evaluation of a New Type of Random Access File Organization' by Montgomery[19]; 'An Indirect Chaining Method for Addressing on Secondary Keys' by Johnson[20]; *Improving the Efficiency of Randomly Organised Files by Loading in Access Frequency Order* by Owen Hanson[21]. Between them, these publications will provide the reader with a very full coverage of direct files.

Indexed-sequential files

The main sources of information here are: *File Organization and Evaluation Modelling Systems (FOREM)* by Lum and Owens[22], in which optimization techniques are described; 'Quantitative File Evaluation and Design' by Montgomery and Hubbard[23], who, following their earlier work, compare IBM and ICL 1900 series software; and 'Modelling of Indexed

Sequential Files: Monitoring Disk Transfers' by Huzan[24], in which she analyzes the operation of ICL 1900 series software in detail.

In 'The Hidden Speed of ISAM', Coyle[25] describes how to optimize ISAM files, based on the work carried out by Coyle on an ISAM file that was causing problems.

Choice between file organizations

Papers in this area include: 'Choosing between Sequentially and Indexed Sequentially Organised Files for Sequential Processing' by Owen Hanson[26]; 'Entry to the File: Randomize or Index' by Kaimann[27]; 'Direct or Indexed Sequential— a File Designer's Guide' by Owen Hanson[28]; and 'Indexed Sequential v Random' by Nijssen[29]. Nijssen's paper concentrates on batch updating of the two types of file; the others cover a wider field, indicated by their titles.

The actual usage figures for file organizations in the UK come from projects by Patel, *Survey on File Organization Techniques in DP Industry*[30], and Woo, *Survey on the Type and Range of Record Key Sequences and File Organization Techniques used in DP Industry*[31].

Database systems

There are so many journal references in this area that books are the most suitable sources of information. Three of the most useful are Date's *Introduction to Database Systems*[32], and Martin's *Computer Database Organization*[33] and *Principles of Database Management*[34]. Specific areas of interest are covered in 'Practical Aspects of Database Systems' by Revell[35]; 'The Impact of Implementing Database Systems in Organisations' by Sherif and Hanson[36]; 'The Database Approach in a Small Systems Environment' by Revell[37]; and the *MDBS User Manual*[38].

On-line systems

The most comprehensive reference here is *Design of Real-Time Computer Systems* by Martin[39]. Other points are made in 'Parallel Programming' by Gilb[40] (also in 'Gilb's mythology', a regular feature in *Computer Weekly*) and in Revell's 'A Survey of Security of On-line Systems in the UK'[41].

Security

A very useful general reference, giving wide coverage at an advanced level, is *Keeping Computers under Control*, edited by Chambers and Hanson[42]. It cites many of the major sources for further study. Martin, in *Security, Accuracy and Privacy in Computer Systems*[43], reviews the whole field, and the National Computer Centre (in the UK) publishes *NCC Programming Standards*[44].

Owen Hanson discusses checkpoints in considerable detail in 'When and How to Use Checkpoints'[45]. In this paper, he cites all the other major sources in the field of checkpointing.

Use and performance of input–output devices

The complete range of secondary storage devices (tapes, disks, disk caches, mass-storage devices, optical disks), the design of secondary storage systems and a review of software aids for secondary storage, are included in *Choosing and Using Secondary Storage*, by Hanson, Revell and others[46]. Information on secondary storage is given in a series of *All about . . .* reports from Datapro[47]. Data on the use of primary input devices is published in the Datapro Report *User Ratings of Key Entry Equipment*[48], in which the relative popularity of all the common input methods is assessed.

References

1. Hanson, O. J., *Design of Computer Data Files*, Pitman, 1982.
2. Walker, E. S., 'Optimization of Tape Operations', *Software Age*, Aug/Sep 1971, pp. 16–17.
3. Waters, S. J., 'Blocking Sequentially Processed Magnetic Files', *Computer Journal*, Vol. 14, No. 2, 1971, pp. 109–112.
4. Inglis, J., and Dee, E. G., 'Flexibility of Block-length for Magnetic Files', *Computer Journal*, Vol. 16, No. 4, 1973, pp. 303–307.
5. Edwards, B. J., 'Choice of Block Sizes for Magnetic Tape Files', *Computer Journal*, Vol. 20, No. 1, 1977, pp. 10–14.
6. Kouvatsos, D. D., and Wong, S. K., 'On Optimum Blocking of Sequential Files', *Computer Journal*, Vol. 27, No. 4, Nov. 1984, pp. 321–327.
7. Hanson, O. J., *Basic File Design*. IPC Electrical and Electronic Press, 1978.
8. Hanson, O. J., 'The Choice between Magnetic Tape and Magnetic Disc for Sequential File Handling', *Proceedings of ADV Kongress*, 1980, Vol. 1, pp. 89–122.
9. Hanson, O. J., *Statistical Searching of Sequential Disc Files*, Working Paper No. 15, The City University Business School. [Obtainable from Librarian, CUBS, The City University, London EC1V 0HB.]
10. Ansari, S., *Performance Evaluation of ICL Disk EDS60 using Sequential File Organization*. MSc Thesis, The City University, 1981. [Obtainable from Librarian, The City University, London EC1V 0HB.]
11. Petersen, W. W., 'Addressing for Random Access Storage', *IBM Journal of Research and Development,* Vol. 1, No. 2, Apr 1957, pp. 130–146.
12. Buchholz, W., 'File Organization and Addressing', *IBM Systems Journal*, Vol. 2, June 1963, pp. 86–111.
13. Lum, V. Y., Yuen, P. S. T., and Dodd, M., 'Key-to-Address Techniques: a Fundamental Performance Study on Large Existing Formatted Files', *CACM*, Vol. 14, No. 4, Apr 1971, pp. 228–239.
14. Kaimann, R. A., *Structured Information Files*, Melville, 1973.
15. Severance, D., and Duhne, R., 'A Practitioner's Guide to Addressing Algorithms', *CACM*, Vol. 19, No. 6, Jun 1976, pp. 314–326.
16. Hanson, O. J., 'Handling Overflows in Direct Files', *Proceedings of Eighth Australian Computer Conference*, 1978, Vol. 2, pp. 662–680.
17. Yaffe, M., *An Evaluation of the Various Parameters affecting the Design of Direct Access Files using Descriptive, Analytical and Simulation Methods*, MSc Thesis, The City University, 1982. [Obtainable from Librarian, The City University, London EC1V 0HB.]

18. Heising, W. P., 'Note on Random Addressing Techniques', *IBM Systems Journal*, June 1963, pp. 112–116.
19. Montgomery, A. Y., 'Algorithms and Performance Evaluation of a New Type of Random Access File Organization', *Australian Computer Journal*, Vol. 6, No. 1, Mar 1974, pp. 3–7.
20. Johnson, L. R., 'An Indirect Chaining Method for Addressing on Secondary Keys', *CACM*, Vol. 14, No. 5, 1961, pp. 218–222.
21. Hanson, O. J., *Improving the Efficiency of Randomly Organised Files by Loading in Access Frequency Order*, Working Paper No. 7, The City University Business School. [Obtainable from Librarian, CUBS, The City University, London EC1V 0HB.]
22. Lum, V. Y., and Owens, P. J., 'File Organization and Evaluation Modelling Systems (FOREM)', Published by IBM, February 1971, pp 146 and Proceedings of IFIP Conference, 1968, Vol. 1, pp. 514–519.
23. Montgomery, A. Y., and Hubbard, D., 'Quantitative File Evaluation and Design', *Proceedings of Eighth Australian Computer Conference*, 1978, Vol. 3, pp. 1242–1266.
24. Huzan, E., 'Modelling of Indexed Sequential Files: Monitoring Disk Transfers', *Computer Journal*, Vol. 22, No. 1, Feb 1979, pp. 22–27
25. Coyle, F. T., 'The Hidden Speed of ISAM', *Datamation*, 15 Jun 1971, pp. 48–49.
26. Hanson, O. J., 'Choosing between Sequentially and Indexed Sequentially Organized Files for Sequential Processing', *Proceedings of Sixth New Zealand Computer Conference*, 1978, Vol. 2, pp. 136–155.
27. Kaimann, R. A., 'Entry to the File: Randomize or Index, Part 1', *Data Processing Magazine*, Vol. 8, No. 12, 1966, pp. 18–21; Part 2, Vol. 10, No. 12, 1968, pp. 24–27.
28. Hanson, O. J., 'Direct or Indexed Sequential—a File Designer's Guide', *Proceedings of Sixth New Zealand Computer Conference*, 1978, Vol. 1, pp. 517–533.
29. Nijssen, G. M., 'Indexed Sequential v Random', *IAG Journal*, Vol. 4, No. 1, 1971, pp. 27–37.
30. Patel, R., *Survey on File Organization Techniques*, Project Paper, The City University Business School, 1982. [Obtainable from Librarian, CUBS, The City University, London EC1V 0HB.]
31. Woo, S. M., *Survey on the Type and Range of Record Key Sequences and File Organization Techniques used in DP Industry*, Project Paper, The City University Business School, 1983. [Obtainable from Librarian, CUBS, The City University, London EC1V 0HB.]
32. Date, C. J., *Introduction to Database Systems*, Third Edition, Addison-Wesley, 1981.
33. Martin, J., *Computer Data-base Organization*, Prentice-Hall, 1977.
34. Martin, J., *Principles of Data-base Management*, Prentice-Hall, 1976.
35. Revell, N., 'Practical Aspects of Database Systems', *Proceedings of International Conference on Computer Applications in Developing Countries*, 1977, pp. 533–550.
36. Sherif, J., and Hanson, O. J., 'The Impact of Implementing Database Systems in Organisations', *Proceedings of Eighth Australian Computer Conference*,

1978, Vol. 4, pp. 1612–1626.

37. Revell, N., 'The Database Approach in Small Systems Environments', *Proceedings of South-East Asian Conference*, 1982, pp. 305–312.
38. *MDBS User Manual*, MDBS Inc.
39. Martin, J., *Design of Real-time Computer Systems*, Prentice-Hall, 1967.
40. Gilb, T., 'Parallel Programming', *Datamation*, Oct 1974, pp. 160–161 [*See also* 'Gilb's Mythodology', regular feature in *Computer Weekly*].
41. Revell, N., 'A Survey of Security of On-line Systems in the UK', *Proceedings of ADV Kongress*, 1978, pp. 397–404.
42. Chambers, A., and Hanson, O. J., (editors), *Keeping Computers under Control*, Gee, 1975.
43. Martin, J., *Security, Accuracy and Privacy in Computer Systems*, Prentice-Hall, 1974.
44. *NCC Programming Standards*, National Computing Centre, 1972.
45. Hanson, O. J., 'When and How to Use Checkpoints', *Proceedings of Ninth Australian Computer Conference*, 1982, Vol. 1, pp. 421–435.
46. Hanson, O. J., *et al.*, *Choosing and Using Secondary Storage*, Xephon Technology Transfer.
47. *All about Plug Compatible Tape Drives; All about Winchester Disk Drives; All about Plug Compatible Disk Drives*, Datapro Reports, Nos. 70-D6-010 on.
48. *User Ratings of Key Entry Equipment*, Datapro Report No. 70-D4-010, 1983.

Appendix: Useful prime numbers

2	3	5	7	11	13	17	19	23	29	31	37
41	43	47	53	59	61	67	71	73	79	83	89
97	101	103	107	109	113	127	131	137	139	149	151
157	163	167	173	179	181	191	193	197	199	211	223
227	229	233	239	241	251	257	263	269	271	277	281
283	293	307	311	313	317	331	337	347	349	353	359
367	373	379	383	389	397	401	409	419	421	431	433
439	443	449	457	461	463	467	479	487	491	499	503
509	521	523	541	547	557	563	569	571	577	587	593
599	601	607	613	617	619	631	641	643	647	653	659
661	673	677	683	691	701	709	719	727	733	739	743
751	757	761	769	773	787	797	809	811	821	823	827
829	839	853	857	859	863	877	881	883	887	907	911
919	929	937	941	947	953	967	971	977	983	991	997
1009	1013	1021	1031	1033	1039	1049	1051	1061	1063	1069	1087
1091	1093	1097	1103	1109	1117	1123	1129	1151	1153	1163	1171
1181	1187	1193	1201	1213	1217	1223	1229	1231	1237	1249	1259
1277	1279	1283	1289	1291	1297	1301	1303	1307	1319	1321	1327
1361	1367	1373	1381	1399	1409	1423	1427	1429	1433	1439	1447
1451	1453	1459	1471	1481	1483	1487	1489	1493	1499	1511	1523
1531	1543	1549	1553	1559	1567	1571	1579	1583	1597	1601	1607
1609	1613	1619	1621	1627	1637	1657	1663	1667	1669	1693	1697
1699	1709	1721	1723	1733	1741	1747	1753	1759	1777	1783	1787
1789	1801	1811	1823	1831	1847	1861	1867	1871	1873	1877	1879
1889	1901	1907	1913	1931	1933	1949	1951	1973	1979	1987	1993
1997	1999	2003	2011	2017	2027	2029	2039	2053	2063	2069	2081
2083	2087	2089	2099	2111	2113	2129	2131	2137	2141	2143	2153
2161	2179	2203	2207	2213	2221	2237	2239	2243	2251	2267	2269
2273	2281	2287	2293	2297	2309	2311	2333	2339	2341	2347	2351
2357	2371	2377	2381	2383	2389	2393	2399	2411	2417	2423	2437
2441	2447	2459	2467	2473	2477	2503	2521	2531	2539	2543	2549
2551	2557	2579	2591	2593	2609	2617	2621	2633	2647	2657	2659
2663	2671	2677	2683	2687	2689	2693	2699	2707	2711	2713	2719
2729	2731	2741	2749	2753	2767	2777	2789	2791	2797	2801	2803
2819	2833	2837	2843	2851	2857	2861	2879	2887	2897	2903	2909
2917	2927	2939	2953	2957	2963	2969	2971	2999	3001	3011	3019
3023	3037	3041	3049	3061	3067	3079	3083	3089	3109	3119	3121
3137	3163	3167	3169	3181	3187	3191	3203	3209	3217	3221	3229
3251	3253	3257	3259	3271	3299	3301	3307	3313	3319	3323	3329
3331	3343	3347	3359	3361	3371	3373	3389	3391	3407	3413	3433
3449	3457	3461	3463	3467	3469	3491	3499	3511	3517	3527	3529
3533	3539	3541	3547	3557	3559	3571	3581	3583	3593	3607	3613
3617	3623	3631	3637	3643	3659	3671	3673	3677	3691	3697	3701
3709	3719	3727	3733	3739	3761	3767	3769	3779	3793	3797	3803
3821	3823	3833	3847	3851	3853	3863	3877	3881	3889	3907	3911
3917	3919	3923	3929	3931	3943	3947	3967	3989	4001	4003	4007
4013	4019	4021	4027	4049	4051	4057	4073	4079	4091	4093	4099
4111	4127	4129	4133	4139	4153	4157	4159	4177	4201	4211	4217
4219	4229	4231	4241	4243	4253	4259	4261	4271	4273	4283	4289
4297	4327	4337	4339	4349	4357	4363	4373	4391	4397	4409	4421
4423	4441	4447	4451	4457	4463	4481	4483	4493	4507	4513	4517
4519	4523	4547	4549	4561	4567	4583	4591	4597	4603	4621	4637
4639	4643	4649	4651	4657	4663	4673	4679	4691	4703	4721	4723
4729	4733	4751	4759	4783	4787	4789	4793	4799	4801	4813	4817
4831	4861	4871	4877	4889	4903	4909	4919	4931	4933	4937	4943
4951	4957	4967	4969	4973	4987	4993	4999	5003	5009	5011	5021
5023	5039	5051	5059	5077	5081	5087	5099	5101	5107	5113	5119
5147	5153	5167	5171	5179	5189	5197	5209	5227	5231	5233	5237
5261	5273	5279	5281	5297	5303	5309	5323	5333	5347	5351	5381
5387	5393	5399	5407	5413	5417	5419	5431	5437	5441	5443	5449
5471	5477	5479	5483	5501	5503	5507	5519	5521	5527	5531	5557
5563	5569	5573	5581	5591	5623	5639	5641	5647	5651	5653	5657
5659	5669	5683	5689	5693	5701	5711	5717	5737	5741	5743	5749
5779	5783	5791	5801	5807	5813	5821	5827	5839	5843	5849	5851
5857	5861	5867	5869	5879	5881	5897	5903	5923	5927	5939	5953
5981	5987	6007	6011	6029	6037	6043	6047	6053	6067	6073	6079
6089	6091	6101	6113	6121	6131	6133	6143	6151	6163	6173	6197
6199	6203	6211	6217	6221	6229	6247	6257	6263	6269	6271	6277
6287	6299	6301	6311	6317	6323	6329	6337	6343	6353	6359	6361
6367	6373	6379	6389	6397	6421	6427	6449	6451	6469	6473	6481
6491	6521	6529	6547	6551	6553	6563	6569	6571	6577	6581	6599
6607	6619	6637	6653	6659	6661	6673	6679	6689	6691	6701	6703
6709	6719	6733	6737	6761	6763	6779	6781	6791	6793	6803	6823
6827	6829	6833	6841	6857	6863	6869	6871	6883	6899	6907	6911
6917	6947	6949	6959	6961	6967	6971	6977	6983	6991	6997	7001
7013	7019	7027	7039	7043	7057	7069	7079	7103	7109	7121	7127
7129	7151	7159	7177	7187	7193	7207	7211	7213	7219	7229	7237
7243	7247	7253	7283	7297	7307	7309	7321	7331	7333	7349	7351
7369	7393	7411	7417	7433	7451	7457	7459	7477	7481	7487	7489
7499	7507	7517	7523	7529	7537	7541	7547	7549	7559	7561	7573

```
7577   7583   7589   7591   7603   7607   7621   7639   7643   7649   7669   7673
7681   7687   7691   7699   7703   7717   7723   7727   7741   7753   7757   7759
7789   7793   7817   7823   7829   7841   7853   7867   7873   7877   7879   7883
7901   7907   7919   7927   7933   7937   7949   7951   7963   7993   8009   8011
8017   8039   8053   8059   8069   8081   8087   8089   8093   8101   8111   8117
8123   8147   8161   8167   8171   8179   8191   8209   8219   8221   8231   8233
8237   8243   8263   8269   8273   8287   8291   8293   8297   8311   8317   8329
8353   8363   8369   8377   8387   8389   8419   8423   8429   8431   8443   8447
8461   8467   8501   8513   8521   8527   8537   8539   8543   8563   8573   8581
8597   8599   8609   8623   8627   8629   8641   8647   8663   8669   8677   8681
8689   8693   8699   8707   8713   8719   8731   8737   8741   8747   8753   8761
8779   8783   8803   8807   8819   8821   8831   8837   8839   8849   8861   8863
8867   8887   8893   8923   8929   8933   8941   8951   8963   8969   8971   8999
9001   9007   9011   9013   9029   9041   9043   9049   9059   9067   9091   9103
9109   9127   9133   9137   9151   9157   9161   9173   9181   9187   9199   9203
9209   9221   9227   9239   9241   9257   9277   9281   9283   9293   9311   9319
9323   9337   9341   9343   9349   9371   9377   9391   9397   9403   9413   9419
9421   9431   9433   9437   9439   9461   9463   9467   9473   9479   9491   9497
9511   9521   9533   9539   9547   9551   9587   9601   9613   9619   9623   9629
9631   9643   9649   9661   9677   9679   9689   9697   9719   9721   9733   9739
9743   9749   9767   9769   9781   9787   9791   9803   9811   9817   9829   9833
9839   9851   9857   9859   9871   9883   9887   9901   9907   9923   9929   9931
9941   9949   9967   9973   10007  10009  10037  10039  10061  10067  10093  10099
10141  10193  10289  10391  10487  10589  10691  10789  10891  10993  11093  11177
11287  11393  11491  11593  11689  11789  11887  11987  12073  12163  12289  12391
12491  12589  12689  12791  12893  12983  13093  13187  13291  13381  13487  13591
13693  13789  13883  13967  14087  14177  14293  14389  14489  14593  14683  14783
14891  14983  15091  15193  15289  15391  15493  15583  15683  15791  15889  15991
16091  16193  16273  16381  16493  16573  16693  16787  16889  16993  17093  17191
17293  17393  17491  17581  17683  17791  17891  17989  18089  18191  18289  18379
18493  18593  18691  18793  18869  18979  19087  19183  19289  19391  19489  19583
19687  19793  19891  19993  20089  20183  20287  20393  20483  20593  20693  20789
20887  20983  21089  21193  21283  21391  21493  21589  21683  21787  21893  21991
22093  22193  22291  22391  22483  22573  22691  22787  22877  22993  23087  23189
23293  23371  23473  23593  23689  23789  23893  23993  24001  24181  24281  24391
24481  24593  24691  24793  24889  24989  25087  25189  25261  25391  25471  25589
25693  25793  25889  25981  26083  26189  26293  26393  26489  26591  26693  26783
26993  27091  27191  27283  27367  27487  27583  27691  27793  27893  27983
28087  28183  28289  28393  28493  28591  28687  28793  28879  28979  29077  29191
29287  29389  29483  29587  29683  29789  29881  29989  30091  30187  30293  30391
30493  30593  30689  30781  30893  30983  31091  31193  31277  31393  31489  31583
31687  31793  31891  31991  32089  32191  32261  32381  32491  32587  32693  32789
32887  32993  33091  33191  33289  33391  33493  33589  33679  33791  33893  33967
34061  34183  34283  34381  34487  34591  34693  34781  34883  34981  35089  35171
35291  35393  35491  35593  35677  35771  35879  35993  36083  36191  36293  36389
36493  36587  36691  36793  36887  36979  37087  37189  37277  37379  37493  37591
37693  37783  37889  37993  38083  38189  38287  38393  38461  38593  38693  38791
38891  38993  39089  39191  39293  39383  39461  39581  39679  39791  39887  39989
40093  40193  40289  40387  40493  40591  40693  40787  40883  40993  41081  41189
41281  41389  41491  41593  41687  41777  41893  41983  42089  42193  42293  42391
42491  42589  42689  42793  42863  42989  43093  43189  43291  43391  43487  43591
43691  43793  43891  43991  44089  44189  44293  44389  44491  44587  44687  44789
44893  44987  45083  45191  45293  45389  45491  45589  45691  45779  45893  45989
46093  46187  46279  46381  46489  46591  46691  46771  46889  46993  47093  47189
47293  47389  47491  47591  47681  47791  47881  47981  49001  48193  48281  48383
48491  48593  48679  48787  48889  48991  49001  49193  49279  49393  49481  49559
49681  49789  49891  49993  50093  50177  50291  50387  50461  50593  50683  50789
50893  50993  51071  51193  51287  51383  51487  51593  51691  51787  51893  51991
52081  52189  52291  52391  52489  52583  52691  52783  52889  52981  53093  53189
53281  53381  53479  53593  53693  53791  53891  53993  54091  54193  54293  54377
54493  54583  54679  54787  54881  54983  55079  55171  55291  55381  55487  55589
55691  55793  55889  55987  56093  56179  56269  56393  56489  56591  56687  56783
56893  56993  57089  57193  57287  57389  57493  57593  57689  57793  57881  57991
58073  58193  58271  58393  58481  58579  58693  58789  58888  58991  59093  59183
59281  59393  59473  59581  59693  59791  59887  59981  60091  60169  60293  60383
60493  60589  60689  60793  60889  60961  61091  61169  61291  61381  61493  61583
61687  61781  61879  61991  62081  62191  62273  62383  62483  62591  62687  62791
62873  62989  63079  63179  63281  63391  63493  63589  63691  63793  63863  63977
64091  64189  64283  64381  64489  64591  64693  64793  64891  64969  65089  65183
65293  65393  65479  65587  65687  65789  65881  65993  66089  66191  66293  66383
66491  66593  66683  66791  66889  66977  67079  67189  67289  67391  67493  67589
67679  67789  67891  67993  68087  68111  68281  68389  68491  68581  68687  68791
68891  68993  69073  69193  69263  69389  69493  69593  69691  69779  69877  69991
70079  70183  70289  70393  70489  70589  70687  70793  70891  70991  71089  71191
71293  71389  71483  71593  71693  71789  71887  71993  72091  72173  72287  72383
72493  72577  72689  72767  72893  72977  73091  73189  73291  73387  73483  73589
73693  73783  73883  73973  74093  74189  74293  74383  74489  74587  74687  74779
74891  74959  75083  75193  75289  75391  75479  75583  75589  75793  75883  75991
76091  76163  76289  76387  76493  76579  76679  76781  76883  76991  77093  77191
77291  77383  77491  77591  77689  77783  77793  77993  78079  78193  78283  78367
78487  78593  78691  78791  78893  78989  79087  79193  79283  79393  79493  79589
79693  79777  79889  79987  80077  80191  80287  80387  80491  80567  80687  80789
80863  80989  81083  81181  81293  81373  81463  81569  81689  81773  81883  81973
```

```
82073  82193  82279  82393  82493  82591  82657  82793  82891  82981  83093  83177
83273  83389  83477  83591  83689  83791  83891  83987  84089  84191  84263  84391
84481  84589  84691  84793  84871  84991  85093  85193  85259  85381  85487  85577
85691  85793  85889  85991  86083  86183  86293  86389  86491  86587  86693  86783
86869  86993  87083  87187  87293  87383  87491  87589  87691  87793  87887  87991
88093  88177  88289  88379  88493  88591  88681  88793  88883  88993  89087  89189
89293  89393  89491  89591  89689  89783  89981  89989  90089  90191  90289  90379
90481  90583  90679  90793  90887  90989  91081  91193  91291  91393  91493  91591
91691  91781  91873  91969  92083  92189  92269  92387  92489  92593  92693  92791
92893  92993  93089  93187  93287  93383  93493  93581  93683  93787  93893  93983
94079  94169  94291  94379  94483  94583  94693  94793  94889  94993  95093  95191
95287  95393  95483  95581  95651  95791  95891  95989  96079  96181  96293  96377
96493  96589  96671  96787  96893  96989  97081  97187  97283  97387  97463  97583
97687  97789  97883  97987  98081  98179  98269  98389  98573  98689  98779
98893  98993  99089  99191  99289  99391  99487  99581  99689  99793  99881  99991
100493 100987 101489 101987 102481 102983 103483 103993 104491 104987 105491 105983
106487 106993 107473 107981 108463 108991 109481 109987 110491 110989 111493 111997
112481 112979 113489 113989 114493 114973 115471 115987 116491 116993 117443 117991
118493 118973 119489 119993 120473 120977 121493 121993 122489 122971 123493 123989
124493 124991 125471 125963 126493 126989 127493 127979 128489 128993 129491 129971
130489 130987 131489 131969 132491 132983 133493 133993 134489 134989 135479 135979
136483 136993 137491 137993 138493 138977 139493 139991 140477 140989 141481 141991
142469 142993 143489 143981 144481 144983 145487 145991 146477 146989 147487 147977
148483 148991 149491 149993 150473 150991 151483 151969 152461 152993 153487 153991
154493 154991 155473 155921 156493 156979 157591 157991 158993 159491 159979
160483 160981 161471 161983 162493 162989 163487 163993 164477 164987 165479 165983
166487 166987 167491 167987 168491 168979 169493 169991 170483 170971 171491 171947
172489 172993 173491 173993 174491 174991 175493 175993 176489 176989 177493 177979
178489 178987 179483 179999 180491 180959 181459 181981 182489 182981 183487 183979
184489 184993 185491 185993 186481 186959 187477 187987 188491 188983 189483 189989
190471 190979 191477 191977 192463 192991 193493 193993 194483 194989 195493 195991
196477 196993 197479 197971 198491 198977 199489 199967 200483 200989 201493 201979
202493 202987 203461 203989 204487 204983 205493 205993 206489 206993 207473 207973
208493 208993 209477 209987 210491 210967 211493 211979 212479 212987 213491 213989
214483 214993 215483 215983 216493 216991 217489 217981 218479 218993 219491 219983
220471 220973 221489 221989 222493 222991 223493 223969 224491 224993 225493 225989
226487 226991 227489 227993 228479 228989 229487 229981 230479 230977 231493 231967
232487 232987 233489 233993 234473 234491 235493 235979 236479 236993 237487 237977
238481 238991 239489 239977 240491 240967 241489 241993 242491 242989 243487 243989
244493 244957 245477 245989 246473 246979 247463 247993 248483 248987 249463 249989
250489 250993 251491 251983 252481 252983 253493 253993 254491 254987 255487 255989
256489 256981 257489 257993 258491 258991 259459 259993 260489 260987 261467 261983
262489 262981 263491 263983 264487 264991 265493 265987 266491 266993 267493 267961
268493 268993 269473 269987 270493 270973 271489 271981 272477 272989 273473 273979
274489 274993 275491 275987 276487 276977 277493 277993 278491 278981 279481 279991
280487 280979 281431 281993 282493 282991 283489 283979 284489 284989 285473 285983
286493 286987 287491 287977 288493 288991 289489 289987 290489 290993 291491 291983
292493 292993 293483 293989 294479 294991 295459 295993 296489 296987 297487 297991
298483 298993 299479 299993 300493 300977 301493 301993 302483 302989 303493 303983
304489 304981 305489 305971 306491 306991 307481 307969 308491 308989 309493 309989
310493 310987 311473 311981 312469 312989 313477 313993 314491 314989 315493 315977
316493 316991 317491 317987 318473 318979 319993 320953 321469 321991
322463 322969 323473 323987 324491 324991 325487 325993 326479 326993 327493 327983
328481 328981 329489 329993 330469 330983 331489 331973 332489 332983 333493 333989
334493 334993 335477 335957 336491 336989 337489 337973 338477 338993 339491 339991
340481 340979 341491 341993 342491 342989 343489 343963 344483 344987 345487 345979
346469 346963 347489 347993 348487 348991 349493 349991 350459 350989 351479 351991
352493 352991 353489 353963 354479 354983 355483 355969 356479 356989 357473 357989
358487 358993 359483 359987 360481 360989 361481 361973 362473 362987 363491 363989
364499 364993 365489 365983 366479 366983 367469 367957 368491 368957 369491 369991
370493 370949 371491 371981 372481 372979 373483 373987 374483 374993 375481 375983
376483 376969 377491 377981 378479 378977 379459 379993 380483 380983 381487 381991
382483 382979 383489 383987 384491 384983 385483 385991 386489 386983 387493 387977
388489 388991 389483 389989 390493 390991 391487 391987 392489 392983 393487 393983
394487 394993 395491 395971 396479 396983 397489 397981 398491 398989 399493 399989
400481 400993 401477 401993 402487 402991 403483 403993 404489 404983 405491 405991
406487 406993 407489 407993 408491 408979 409483 409993 410491 410983 411491 411991
412493 412987 413477 413981 414487 414991 415489 415993 416491 416989 417493 417991
418493 418993 419491 419959 420481 420977 421493 421987 422479 422489 423481 423991
424493 424967 425489 425989 426481 426973 427477 427993 428489 428977 429487 429991
430487 430987 431479 431993 432491 432989 433471 433981 434479 434989 435481 435983
436483 436993 437473 437977 438047 438091 438143 438169 438241 438287 438341 438391
438479 438989 439493 439991 440471 440509 441479 441971 442489 442981 443489 443987
444487 444979 445477 445969 446473 446987 447481 447991 448451 448993 449473 449989
450493 450991 451481 451987 452453 452989 453461 453991 454483 454991 455491 455993
456461 456991 457469 457987 458483 458993 459479 459961 460477 460991 461479 461983
462493 462983 463483 463993 464399 464993 465469 465983 466483 466957 467491 467977
468493 468983 469487 469993 470489 470993 471487 471959 472477 472993 473479 473987
474491 474983 475483 475991 476489 476989 477491 477977 478493 478993 479489 479911
480463 480989 481489 481963 482483 482971 483491 483991 484493 484987 485479 485993
486491 486989 487489 487979 488473 488993 489493 489989 490493 490993 491489 491983
492491 492979 493481 493993 494471 494987 495491 495983 496493 496963 497491 497993
498493 498989 499493 499979 500483 500977 501493 501971 502487 502973 503483 503989
```

```
504479  504991  505493  505979  506491  506993  507491  507979  508489  508987  509477  509989
510481  510989  511487  511991  512467  512989  513481  513991  514453  514967  515477  515993
516493  516991  517487  517991  518473  518989  519487  519989  520451  520981  521491  521993
522479  522989  523493  523987  524453  524983  525493  525983  526483  526993  527489  527993
528491  528991  529489  529987  530447  530989  531481  531989  532489  532993  533459  533993
534491  534971  535489  535991  536491  536989  537413  537991  538487  538987  539479  539993
540469  540989  541483  541993  542489  542987  543463  543971  544487  544979  545483  545959
546479  546977  547493  547957  548489  548963  549481  549991  550489  550993  551489  551981
552493  552991  553481  553991  554467  554977  555491  555967  556487  556987  557489  557987
558491  558979  559483  559991  560491  560977  561461  561983  562493  562987  563489  563987
564491  564989  565489  565979  566453  566987  567493  567991  568493  568991  569479  569983
570491  570991  571477  571973  572491  572993  573493  573977  574493  574969  575489  575987
576493  576977  577483  577981  578489  578971  579473  579983  580487  580981  581491  581983
582469  582983  583489  583991  584473  584993  585493  585989  586493  586981  587473  587989
588493  588977  589493  589993  590489  590987  591469  591973  592489  592993  593491  593993
594469  594989  595481  595981  596489  596987  597473  597967  598489  598987  599491  599993
600487  600983  601487  601981  602489  602983  603487  603989  604481  604973  605477  605993
606493  606971  607493  607993  608483  608989  609487  609991  610469  610993  611483  611993
612481  612977  613493  613993  614483  614983  615493  615971  616489  616991  617479  617983
618463  618991  619477  619987  620491  620981  621473  621983  622493  622987  623477  623989
624487  624983  625489  625979  626489  626987  627491  627973  628493  628993  629491  629989
630493  630967  631487  631993  632483  632993  633487  633991  634493  634979  635483  635989
636473  636983  637489  637939  638489  638993  639493  639983  640483  640993  641491  641981
642487  642977  643493  643991  644491  644977  645493  645979  646453  646993  647489  647987
648481  648971  649487  649991  650483  650987  651487  651971  652493  652991  653491  653993
654491  654991  655489  655987  656483  656987  657493  657983  658487  658991  659473  659983
660493  660983  661483  661993  662491  662957  663463  663991  664471  664973  665479  665993
666493  666989  667487  667991  668471  668989  669481  669989  670493  670991  671477  671981
672493  672983  673487  673991  674483  674987  675481  675979  676493  676993  677473  677983
678493  678989  679487  679993  680489  680993  681493  681983  682489  682967  683489  683983
684493  684989  685493  685991  686479  686993  687481  687977  688477  688993  689467  689987
690493  690953  691489  691991  692467  692983  693493  693989  694487  694987  695491  695939
696491  696991  697481  697993  698491  698983  699493  699967  700471  700993  701489  701969
702469  702991  703489  703991  704477  704993  705493  705989  706487  706987  707467  707983
708493  708991  709469  709991  710491  710989  711479  711983  712493  712981  713491  713987
714487  714991  715489  715979  716491  716981  717491  717989  718493  718973  719483  719989
720491  720991  721481  721991  722489  722983  723493  723977  724487  724993  725479  725993
726487  726991  727487  727981  728489  728993  729493  729991  730487  730993  731483  731981
732493  732971  733489  733991  734479  734971  735491  735983  736471  736993  737483  737981
738487  738989  739493  739969  740483  740989  741493  741991  742457  742993  743447  743989
744493  744977  745477  745993  746483  746989  747493  747991  748487  748987  749471  749993
750487  750983  751481  751987  752489  752993  753483  753983  754489  754993  755483  755977
756467  756971  757487  757993  758491  758987  759461  759973  760489  760993  761489  761993
762491  762989  763493  763967  764491  764993  765481  765979  766487  766967  767489  767957
768491  768983  769487  769987  770491  770993  771481  771973  772493  772991  773491  773989
774491  774959  775477  775987  776483  776987  777479  777989  778469  778993  779489  779993
780469  780991  781493  781987  782493  782993  783487  783953  784489  784981  785483  785963
786491  786983  787489  787993  788479  788993  789493  789979  790481  790991  791489  791993
792487  792991  793493  793981  794491  794993  795491  795983  796493  796981  797473  797987
798487  798961  799489  799993  800483  800993  801487  801989  802471  802987  803483  803989
804493  804989  805487  805991  806483  806993  807473  807973  808481  808993  809487  809993
810493  810989  811493  811991  812491  812969  813493  813991  814493  814991  815491  815989
816469  816971  817483  817987  818473  818977  819487  819991  820489  820991  821489  821993
822433  822989  823481  823993  824489  824983  825491  825991  826493  826979  827473  827989
828449  828977  829469  829993  830483  830989  831481  831983  832493  832987  833491  833977
834487  834991  835489  835993  836491  836971  837467  837979  838483  838993  839491  839981
840491  840991  841459  841987  842489  842993  843487  843911  844489  844957  845491  845989
846493  846983  847493  847993  848489  848993  849481  849991  850481  850979  851491  851971
852463  852989  853493  853981  854479  854993  855467  855989  856487  856993  857471  857981
858479  858989  859493  859987  860479  860993  861493  861979  862493  862991  863491  863983
864491  864989  865493  865993  866477  866969  867487  867991  868493  868993  869489  869989
870491  870983  871477  871993  872479  872959  873469  873991  874487  874987  875491  875983
876481  876971  877449  877949  878489  878989  879493  879979  880487  880993  881479  881987
882491  882979  883489  883991  884491  884987  885487  885991  886493  886993  887483  887989
888493  888989  889489  889963  890467  890993  891493  891991  892481  892987  893489  893989
894451  894973  895471  895987  896491  896983  897473  897983  898493  898987  899491  899981
900491  900983  901489  901993  902483  902987  903493  903979  904489  904987  905491  905963
906487  906973  907493  907969  908491  908993  909481  909977  910471  910981  911459  911969
912491  912991  913487  913981  914491  914991  915487  915991  916473  916973  917471  917993
918481  918989  919447  919979  920477  920971  921491  921989  922489  922993  923471  923987
924493  924967  925487  925987  926483  926983  927491  927973  928471  928979  929483  929983
930491  930991  931487  931991  932483  932983  933479  933979  934489  934981  935489  935971
936493  936967  937481  937991  938491  938989  939487  939989  940483  940993  941491  941989
942479  942983  943477  943967  944491  944977  945481  945983  946489  946993  947483  947987
948487  948989  949477  949987  950483  950993  951491  951967  952487  952981  953483  953987
954491  954991  955489  955993  956477  956993  957433  957991  958487  958993  959489  959969
960493  960991  961487  961993  962477  962993  963491  963979  964463  964981  965491  965989
966491  966991  967493  967979  968479  968987  969481  969989  970493  970987  971491  971993
972493  972991  973487  973993  974489  974989  975493  975991  976489  976991  977447  977971
978491  978973  979481  979987  980491  980963  981493  981983  982493  982981  983491  983993
984491  984959  985493  985993  986477  986989  987491  987991  988489  988979  989479  989981
990487  990989  991493  991987  992461  992983  993493  993983  994489  994991  995471  995989
996487  996979  997463  997991  998471  998989  999491  999563  999683  999773  999883  999983
```

Index

Definitions of terms are shown in bold type.